CAMBRIDGE TEXTS IN THE
HISTORY OF PHILOSOPHY

═══

PLATO
Meno and *Phaedo*

CAMBRIDGE TEXTS IN THE
HISTORY OF PHILOSOPHY

Series editors

KARL AMERIKS
Professor of Philosophy, University of Notre Dame

DESMOND M. CLARKE
Emeritus Professor of Philosophy, University College Cork

The main objective of Cambridge Texts in the History of Philosophy is to expand the range, variety, and quality of texts in the history of philosophy which are available in English. The series includes texts by familiar names (such as Descartes and Kant) and also by less well-known authors. Wherever possible, texts are published in complete and unabridged form, and translations are specially commissioned for the series. Each volume contains a critical introduction together with a guide to further reading and any necessary glossaries and textual apparatus. The volumes are designed for student use at undergraduate and postgraduate level, and will be of interest not only to students of philosophy but also to a wider audience of readers in the history of science, the history of theology, and the history of ideas.

For a list of titles published in the series, please see end of book.

PLATO

Meno and *Phaedo*

EDITED BY

DAVID SEDLEY
University of Cambridge

ALEX LONG
University of St Andrews

CAMBRIDGE
UNIVERSITY PRESS

CAMBRIDGE
UNIVERSITY PRESS

University Printing House, Cambridge CB2 8BS, United Kingdom

One Liberty Plaza, 20th Floor, New York, NY 10006, USA

477 Williamstown Road, Port Melbourne, VIC 3207, Australia

314-321, 3rd Floor, Plot 3, Splendor Forum, Jasola District Centre, New Delhi - 110025, India

79 Anson Road, #06-04/06, Singapore 079906

Cambridge University Press is part of the University of Cambridge.

It furthers the University's mission by disseminating knowledge in the pursuit of education, learning and research at the highest international levels of excellence.

www.cambridge.org
Information on this title: www.cambridge.org/9780521859479

© Cambridge University Press 2010

First published 2011
7th printing 2016

A catalogue record for this publication is available from the British Library

Library of Congress Cataloging in Publication data
Plato.
[Meno. English]
Meno ; and, Phaedo / Plato ; edited by David Sedley ; translated by Alex Long.
p. cm. – (Cambridge texts in the history of philosophy)
Includes bibliographical references and index.
ISBN 978-0-521-85947-9 – ISBN 978-0-521-67677-9 (pbk.)
I. Socrates. I. Sedley, D. N. II. Plato. Phaedo. English.
III. Title. IV. Title: Phaedo. V. Series.
B377.A5L55 2010
184 – dc22 2010029488

ISBN 978-0-521-85947-9 Hardback
ISBN 978-0-521-67677-9 Paperback

Contents

Preface

The translations and the 'Further Reading' were drafted by Alex Long, the introduction by David Sedley. The subsequent revision of the whole, and the footnotes to the translation, were shared between the two.

We are most grateful for the advice, criticism and encouragement of Hilary Gaskin of Cambridge University Press, and Desmond Clarke, general editor of the series.

Introduction

Plato's progress

Socrates (469–399 BC) was the first great Athenian philosopher. His pupil
Plato (427/424–347 BC) was the second. Socrates, who left nothing in
writing, was a charismatic but also provocative public figure on the streets
of Athens, raising deep ethical questions with all and sundry, and thereby
spawning both adulators and sworn enemies. The final victory of his
enemies, who secured his conviction and execution at the age of 70,
also marked his canonization as a philosophical guru and martyr. Over
the following hundred years and more, numerous philosophers set out
to resume and complete the project which Socrates was seen as having
initiated. Among these, it was Plato who stood out, both as an incompa-
rably great prose writer and as arguably the most seminal of all ancient
thinkers, even if his own pupil Aristotle could compete for this latter
title. Plato's philosophical writings were mainly in the form of dialogues
and, unusually for an ancient Greek author, they have survived in their
entirety.

Although we know Plato's dates with some precision, have good evidence that the *Laws* was his last work, and can group a few other dialogues
near the end of his life because of their stylistic similarity to the *Laws*,
we have no reliable indicators of date for the great majority of his works,
including the *Meno* and *Phaedo*. Nevertheless, a global chronological
reconstruction has, at least in outline, enjoyed an impressive degree of
consensus for many decades, and this chronology will be assumed in what
follows. The *Meno* and the *Phaedo* (almost certainly written in that order)
are seen as straddling a period in which Plato's philosophical style was

ix

undergoing important changes, namely the transition from his 'early' to his 'middle' period. A reasonable guess would place this phase in the 380s–370s BC.

Plato's preceding dialogues (including *Apology*, *Crito*, *Euthyphro*, *Protagoras*, *Charmides*, *Lysis*) had represented above all his attempt to capture and explore the philosophical persona and significance of Socrates. The ideas which Socrates had been shown exploring there had centred on the nature of human goodness or virtue (*aretē*) as a supremely beneficial state of soul, quite possibly identifiable as a special kind of knowledge, and on a related question, how the specific virtues can be successfully defined. These dialogues typically involved Socrates quizzing an interlocutor, and most ended negatively, with the (ideally at least) cathartic realization of ignorance which Plato at this date saw as the principal pay-off of a Socratic conversation. But there is little doubt that the agenda pursued in these texts, whatever it may have owed to the historical Socrates, was also becoming an integral part of Plato's own philosophy.

The next phase of Plato's work, often called his 'middle' period, is one in which constructive metaphysical speculation and argument take centre stage. Socrates is by now presented as wedded to a hypothesis about the nature of true being: the objects of intellectual inquiries like those pursued in previous dialogues are in fact Forms, the pure essences of beauty, goodness and the like, and these, because their purity means their existing apart from the sensible world, must be found by intellectual activity independent of the senses. This is Plato's celebrated theory of Forms, the capital letter being conventionally used to mark a transcendent as opposed to an immanent property or entity. From another perspective, it has sometimes been called the 'two-world theory', since it turns on a radical division between the sensible and intelligible worlds. It is found in outline in the *Cratylus* and *Symposium*, plays a vital role in the arguments of the *Phaedo*, appears in its most elaborate form in books 5–7 and 10 of the *Republic*, recurs in mythical dress in the *Phaedrus*, and is subjected to searching (though not necessarily fatal) criticism from Plato's own pen in the opening part of the *Parmenides*. All these dialogues, perhaps even written in the order just cited, can be counted as belonging to Plato's middle period, although the *Parmenides* is seen as marking the transition to his final phase. In his late work the theory puts in just one unambiguous further appearance, in the *Timaeus*. The *Meno* does not overtly anticipate the theory even in passages where it might have done (although it says nothing incompatible with it), and this is a ground for regarding it as prior, albeit transitional, to the middle period.

In addition to the theory of Forms, Plato's middle period is marked by an enhanced interest in the immortality of the soul. This thesis becomes the central contention of the *Phaedo*. It also plays an important supporting role in the *Meno*, where, in partial anticipation of the *Phaedo*, it is invoked to underpin Plato's most startling new theory, that all learning is in reality recollection of truths which our souls learnt before their present incarnation. This theory of Recollection constitutes the most direct link between our two dialogues. Indeed, the *Phaedo*'s recapitulation (73a–b) of the *Meno*'s argument for Recollection is one of the few unambiguous intertextual references in the Platonic corpus.

The 'soul' (Greek *psychē*) is a major player in both dialogues. Greek usage makes it natural for Plato to use the term *psychē* both of the mind, where reasoning and virtues can be assumed to reside, and of that element or aspect of us that survives death, if indeed any does. That we do in fact have a *psychē* is uncontroversial to a Greek ear, in a way that does not correspond to modern assumptions about a 'soul'. The latter translation should therefore be recognized as only an approximation to the meaning of this key Greek term.

As the *Meno* opens it is recognizably Plato's early Socrates, more an open-minded inquirer than a constructive theorist, who features as protagonist. Asked whether virtue is the sort of thing that can be taught, he professes total ignorance even of what virtue is and, with a touch of his characteristic irony (deferral to the supposed superior wisdom of others), invites his interlocutor Meno to enlighten him. The result is a cross-examination in which Meno is repeatedly forced to admit confusion, and to withdraw his proffered definitions one after another. However, in the central section of the dialogue a radically new style of Platonic discourse intrudes. It is here that Socrates unveils the theory of Recollection, and even purports to prove its truth by questioning a slave in such a way as to reveal his innate understanding of geometry. This is the precise point in the Platonic corpus at which, according to a common perception, middle-period thought first enters.

However, another prominent feature of the *Meno*, and one that this time unifies its opening and middle sections, is the use of mathematics as a paradigm of knowledge. This is thought not to be part of Plato's Socratic heritage, and may rather reflect the incipient influence of Pythagoreanism. The ambition of making ethics as pure and exact a science as geometry is plainly visible in the *Meno*. The introduction of Forms as the true objects of ethical inquiry is, when it occurs in other dialogues, symptomatic of that same project.

The above should suffice to indicate the transitional character of the *Meno*. It is now time to turn to the dialogue itself.

The *Meno*

Opening conversation

The conversation takes place in Athens in 402 BC, just three years before Socrates' death as portrayed in the *Phaedo*, and the subtly menacing participation in it of Anytus, destined to be one of Socrates' accusers at his trial, reminds us of this proximity. The main interlocutor, Meno, is a wealthy young Thessalian, currently staying with Anytus, and undoubtedly known to Plato's contemporary readers to have ahead of him a morally disreputable military career soon ending in a not-undeservedly grisly death.

The main topic, whether or not virtue is the sort of thing to be acquired by teaching,[1] locates this dialogue in familiar Socratic territory. In fact, it marks the *Meno* as in effect a continuation of the *Protagoras*, where a debate on the same topic between Socrates and the sophist Protagoras ended inconclusively.[2] The main interlocutor this time is not a sophist, but he is a committed disciple of the sophist Gorgias.

Aretē, here rendered 'virtue' (though some prefer 'excellence'), often functions as the Greek abstract noun corresponding to *agathos*, 'good'. It also serves as the generic name for a set of specific virtues especially prized by ancient Greek civic culture, notably wisdom, justice, courage, temperance and piety, these five (or at least the first four) being later known as the 'cardinal virtues'. Athens was a magnet for sophists like Protagoras, professional intellectuals who hired themselves out to teach

---

[1] The question, as we translate it, is whether virtue is 'teachable'. The Greek *didakton* can also be translated 'something taught', the question not, however, being whether it is in fact taught, but whether it is the sort of thing whose transmission is via teaching.

[2] Another area of common ground is that both *Protagoras* (352a–357c) and *Meno* (77b–78b) defend the Socratic paradox that it is impossible to act against knowledge of what is best.

all the skills of citizenship, and it was above all they who professed to be teachers of virtue. Those sophistic pretensions will come under scrutiny in the later part of the dialogue (88c–92e).

Socrates himself, as famously portrayed in Plato's *Apology*, sees his interrogative practice as a divinely assigned mission, that of making his fellow-Athenians better or more virtuous by provoking them to reflect on their moral presuppositions. But he does not claim to 'teach' virtue, and in fact the *Meno* will provide a theoretical rationale for that avoidance (81c–82a): all a 'teacher' can do in reality is ask questions which bring to the surface knowledge already latent in the soul.

But even that diagnosis of teaching will rely on virtue's being the sort of thing – perhaps knowledge, perhaps just true opinion – that could in principle be recalled. And the opening part of the dialogue (70a–79e) is indeed concerned with this primary question, what virtue itself is. For, as Socrates remarks, the definitional question would have to be settled first, before they could meaningfully proceed to the further question whether or not virtue is acquired by teaching.

This opening move appeals to a highly Socratic principle, the Priority of Definition. It is disputed how far the principle is simply one of good method, how far Plato's Socrates thinks that without a definition a term cannot be understood; and, if the latter, whether he means that an undefined term is not yet *philosophically or scientifically* understood, or that it defies even ordinary lexical understanding. The clues in the *Meno* direct us to both ends of this spectrum. On the one hand, Socrates' claim of ignorance is a strong one. He does not even 'know at all' what virtue is; and, he adds (71b), 'how could I know what sort of thing something is, when I don't know what it is? Or do you think that, if someone doesn't know at all who Meno is, it is possible for him to know whether Meno is beautiful or rich?' Both the wording and the analogy suggest that, in the absence of a definition, Socrates doubts if he has even identified virtue correctly yet. On the other hand, he will later praise Meno with the words 'Even if someone had his head covered, Meno, he could tell from your conversation that you're beautiful' (76b), thus pointedly casting doubt on the very analogy – you cannot know whether Meno is beautiful when you do not even know who he is – which earlier supported his appeal to the Priority of Definition. This is one of many subtle ways in which Plato can in the *Meno* be seen critically re-evaluating his own Socratic legacy. He is informally opening the door to a methodology (to be further developed at 86d–87c as a method of 'hypothesis') which will permit the definitional stage of an inquiry to be bypassed.

Nevertheless, the definitional inquiry is initially allowed to run its course (71c–79e), and it is pursued with greater subtlety than in any dialogue likely to predate the *Meno*. Two particular themes are worth noting in this section.

First, when he first offers his own definition of virtue, Meno's mistake (71e–72a) is to reply with a list: the virtue of a man is this, the virtue of a woman is that, and so on. Socrates' reply amounts to a defence of the Unity of Definition: however heterogeneous the items that fall under a universal term, there must be *some* unifying property that entitles them all to the same name. Although Meno resists so far as regards the diversity of virtue, he concedes the point for 'bee', 'health', 'largeness' and 'strength': men and women are healthy, large or strong in the same way, but not *good* in the same way. This contrast implicitly introduces a key point of Platonic method. Beekeeping, medicine, measurement and athletic training are already successful disciplines, which therefore draw on secure data. Goodness belongs to the as yet undeveloped science of ethics. Many philosophers have explained the difference in terms of the different kind of subject matter ethics deals with: values, not facts, for example, or alternatively, in a distinction popular in Plato's own day, 'conventional, not natural'. But for Plato, goodness and other values *are* matters of natural fact, just extraordinarily difficult fact, whose science is still in its infancy.

The other aspect to notice is Plato's new awareness of the dangers of regress and circularity in the definitional process. First, regress. Socrates favours a purely mathematical definition of his specimen definiendum, shape: 'the limit of a solid' (76a, e).[3] If shape, a mathematical concept, is instead defined as 'that which always accompanies colour' (75b), colour too may have to be defined, and unsatisfactorily so if its definition relies on an unconfirmed scientific theory that falls outside the original domain

---

[3] In the *Meno*, 'shape' (*schēma*) appears to be used exclusively for the shape of a 'solid' (see 76a), and not for the outline of a two-dimensional figure or (e.g. 82b) 'area' (*chōrion*). If it were assumed to cover the latter as well, we might have to follow Dominic Scott, *Plato's Meno* (Cambridge, 2006), 35–41 in translating 'surface' instead. But 'straight' and 'round', both called *schēma* (at 75a), are species of shape, not surface, and we have preferred to retain the traditional translation.

of inquiry (75c, 76a–e). One danger of such reliance is subtly put on display. Socrates experimentally adopts a definition of colour which he knows Meno will approve, because it rests on the authority of the physicist Empedocles, endorsed by Empedocles' follower Gorgias and therefore also in turn by Gorgias' follower Meno: 'colour is effluence of shapes, commensurate with sight and thus perceptible' (76d). But if colour is effluence of shapes, in other words if shapes flow from external bodies to the eye, we may wonder how shape could still be 'the limit of a solid'.[4]

Chains of definitions are here threatening to form a regress which, if not infinite, risks at any rate being as weak as its weakest member, and in which systematic consistency is at risk. Socrates' preferred mathematical definition of shape, in accordance with the best principles of dialectic (the method of constructive question-and-answer inquiry), contains no regress-threatening disputed term on which the participants are not already agreed (75c–76a), and stays within the bounds of its own well-established discipline, in this case solid geometry. Plato's confidence that ethical method can learn from mathematics is still in full evidence here.

The above issue crops up in the course of discussing Meno's second definition (73c). The parallel danger of circularity, for its part, looms in the critique of Meno's third definition (77b–79e). His new definition is agreed to amount to 'Virtue is proficiency at securing good things', but he concedes that for completeness 'justly', 'piously' and 'temperately' would have to be added (it could hardly be virtue to secure good things in an unjust or impious way). But thereupon the definition is vitiated, because justice, piety, etc. are agreed to be parts of virtue, parts which we therefore could not be expected to understand unless we *already* knew what virtue itself is. A little reflection may reveal that Meno's previous definitions already looked vulnerable to this circularity objection (73a–b, d), and Plato may be inviting us to wonder how *any* definition of virtue could escape it. His own provisional suggestion will be that virtue is a kind of knowledge (87c–89a), and in other dialogues (*Euthydemus* 291e–293a;

---

[4] An alternative translation of 76d makes colour 'an effluence *from* [not 'of'] shapes'. That would simply substitute a new inconsistency: shape could no longer be 'that which always accompanies colour' (75b).

Republic 6.505b–c) versions even of that thesis are treated as vulnerable to the circularity objection.

Stalemate

At all events, it is at precisely this point that the search for a definition is dropped. Meno expresses his despair as to how the mind-numbingly negative outcome of a Socratic cross-examination could ever be avoided (79e–81a). Socrates replies that he is himself merely communicating his own puzzlement, and proposes that the two of them should seek an answer together. But Meno has been ironically seduced by Socrates into thinking that he himself really knows the answer, and that Socrates has merely made him look as if he does not (80d); so when (at 80d) he proceeds to propound his paradox, famous today as 'Meno's paradox', it is presented as a problem merely about Socrates' predicament:[5] how can Socrates either determine what he is going to look for, or recognize it if he should happen to find it, given that he does not know at all what it is? It is Socrates himself who then converts this into a universal dilemma about inquiry (80e):

> A person turns out not to be able to search either for what he knows or for what he doesn't know? For he wouldn't be searching for what he knows, since he knows it, and someone like that, at least, has no need to search; nor would he be searching for what he doesn't know, since in that case he doesn't even know what to search for.

This reformulation omits what in the end proves to be the most important part of Meno's original paradox, his question how Socrates will know when he has found the right answer.[6] Curiously Meno, in his self-satisfied conviction that he himself already knows what virtue is and merely needs to remove his superficial confusion, is close to Plato's own solution to this problem. For that solution, to which we must now turn, is that thanks to the soul's pre-existence we were born already possessing the knowledge we seek, and that by proper interrogation we can bring it back to the surface.

[5] It usually goes unnoticed that in 'And how will you search for something, Socrates, if you don't know at all what it is?' etc. (80d) 'you' almost certainly does not have the generalizing sense that English 'you' can have, but refers to Socrates alone.
[6] See Scott, *Plato's Meno*, ch. 7.

Recollection

The theory of Recollection, which Socrates proceeds to outline, is developed with the following components:

(a) A religious doctrine (81a–c), attributed to the authority of priests, priestesses and poets. The soul is immortal, and transmigrates between incarnate and discarnate existences. This has enabled it to learn everything.
(b) An epistemological doctrine (81c–e), put forward in Socrates' own voice. Thanks to its pre-existence, a soul can recollect knowledge which it once actively had; and because 'all nature is akin', one such recollection can lead on eventually to global recall. The process we call seeking and learning is in reality just this recollection.
(c) A practical demonstration of (b) (81e–85b). One of Meno's slaves, who it is confirmed has never studied geometry, is taken by Socrates through the problem of constructing a square with twice the area of a given square, helped by diagrams (see pp. 16–22). After a series of wrong answers, whose error becomes clear to him, the slave arrives at the right answer. Yet Socrates claims to have done nothing more than ask him questions throughout.
(d) Reflections on what has been achieved and its implications (85b–86c). True opinions (along with a number of false ones) were already present in the slave. These have now been stirred up. And 'if someone questions him about these things on many occasions and in many ways', he will end up having full knowledge of them. That knowledge will be being retrieved from inside him, i.e. recollected. Moreover, he could extend the same retrieval to the whole of mathematics. Additionally, a byproduct of the demonstration is confirmation that the soul is immortal; but the only conclusion Socrates will absolutely insist on is that confidence in the possibility of seeking and finding knowledge is justified, and is preferable to the lazy alternative of capitulating to Meno's paradox. Socrates and Meno can therefore if they wish resume their search for what virtue is.

It is natural to question the legitimacy of Socrates' cross-questioning procedure: are his questions too leading, for example, and does the slave derive some of his answers from the visual evidence of the diagram rather than from reasoning, or from prior mathematical learning? No doubt corners are cut, if only in the literary interests of reasonable brevity. But one might nevertheless conclude that at the heart of the demonstration stands a key insight: at least in the paradigmatic case of mathematics, knowledge really is attained by searching in one's own inner resources. It is easier to disagree with Socrates' further assumption that those inner resources take the form of latent, prenatally acquired knowledge, and not, for example, just an innate rational capacity. But the underlying insight that mathematical knowledge is (roughly speaking) *a priori*, is itself a significant step towards a quintessentially Platonic thesis, to be fully articulated in the *Republic*: that real knowledge is independent of the senses, and instead has as its objects the occupants of a distinct intelligible world.

Even leaving aside such moves toward Platonism, the theory and its exposition play an important part in Plato's habitual Socratic agenda. First of all, it justifies dialectic, the method of inquiry through question and answer that Socrates had bequeathed. The regular failure of the definitional inquiries in earlier dialogues naturally enough suggested doubts as to how such inquiries could *ever* succeed, given that neither party to the dialectic was already in possession of the answer. Meno's paradox, even though Socrates calls it 'eristic' (80e) (that is, argumentatively confrontational), is in fact a serious encapsulation of this very problem. And Socrates' geometrical demonstration is an equally serious reply: even those with no awareness of the answer to a question may legitimately seek it by raising and answering questions, and can expect to recognize it when they eventually hit upon it.

Admittedly there is a further question, not addressed here by Socrates, as to whether the *a priori* character which makes mathematical knowledge suitable for this treatment extends to moral values as well. On no credible interpretation can Socrates mean that literally *all* learning is achieved in this way, including for example the acquisition of geographical or historical information. The method is clearly tailored to the discovery of *a priori* truths – truths which, on reflection, we realize could not have been otherwise. And there is every reason to think that Plato sees grounds for extending it beyond mathematics to all the theoretical disciplines covered by philosophical dialectic, ethics included.

Not only does the theory of Recollection suggest that the Socratic philosophical method could, given time, arrive at ethical truths, it also gives a specific role to the refutative part of dialectic in which Socrates specialized. The slave passes through the following stages: (1) confidently giving wrong answers, (2) seeing his error, (3) being reduced to numbed puzzlement, (4) making a new start, and (5) finally seeing the right answer. Here the quintessentially Socratic stages (1) to (3) pointedly mirror the stages through which Meno has already passed, and in particular the slave's reduction from confident false belief to a state of numbed puzzlement (82b–84c) is designed to mimic in detail Meno's deflation in the first part of the dialogue (71e–80d). Yet when the slave has been thus humbled, Socrates asks 'So when we made him puzzled and numb, ... we didn't do him any harm, did we?' (84b). The point is that the slave *had* to go through this stage, by being disabused of his previous confident misconceptions, before he would be ready to find out the truth. By analogy, Meno too has not been harmed, but benefited, by his reduction to puzzlement, and for precisely the same reason.

Note too that the numbing effect suffered by Meno is said to be the same one that Socrates has on people quite generally (80a–d). At a second level of subtext, then, what applies singly to Socrates' treatment of Meno applies equally to Socrates' lifetime mission at Athens. His project, devoted to the systematic refutation of false beliefs, was a necessary phase in the history of philosophy. By means of it he has removed enough prevailing misconceptions to make people's minds for the first time ready for the recognition of the truth, and more specifically, we may suppose, for the arrival of Platonism.

The inquiry into virtue renewed

At 86c–d Socrates proposes that they should resume their search for the definition of virtue, but this time he agrees to Meno's request to take a short cut and proceed directly to the secondary question, is virtue the sort of thing to be acquired by teaching? We have already seen (pp. xiii–xiv) Socrates' informal hint, via an analogy, that this reversal of the usual procedure might be justified. He now adds a formal analogy in favour of the same conclusion (86e–87b). Significantly, it once again involves treating geometry, an already successful science, as the model for the future science of ethics. Geometers, Socrates points out, sometimes use a method of 'hypothesis' to solve a problem, and in doing so they are drawing the consequences of some proposition that they do not know in advance to be true. He proposes to use an analogous hypothesis in order to find out whether virtue is teachable despite not already knowing what virtue is.

This time, by contrast with the interrogation of the slave, the chosen mathematical example is both condensed and obscure. Plato may want to convey that, whereas just now the slave was having his first elementary lesson in geometry, at the upper end of the same scale professional geometry is a highly demanding intellectual discipline suitable for an elite, and one such as might provide a transition to the even more demanding science of ethics. Geometry, as a bridge discipline, is being sketched at both its entry and its exit level. We need not, then, press the mathematical details in the expectation that clarity will emerge.[7]

The unclarity of the geometrical 'hypothesis' also infects the ensuing ethical argument which is said to imitate it. What is a 'hypothesis'? It seems that by this term Socrates means any thesis adopted provisionally in order to explore its consequences, and that a typical, although not the only, form that this may take is as the 'If . . . ' clause of a conditional. The two hypotheses he proceeds to invoke are (i) 'Virtue is good' (87d) and (ii) 'Virtue is knowledge' (87b). Although, by Socrates' principles, in the absence of a definition of virtue both propositions must necessarily remain hypothetical, (i) defies disbelief, and the main burden of the argument is to show that (ii) follows from it (87d–89a). Given that (ii) does follow, it itself in turn then functions as a hypothesis: it has after all been inferred from a hypothetical premise, and from it in turn is inferred the provisional conclusion that virtue is teachable. For, as Socrates remarks, if and only if virtue is knowledge is it subject to teaching (87b–c, 89c).

The showpiece of this section is the inference from (i) to (ii), which along with *Euthydemus* 278e–282d is a classic defence of the Socratic thesis that virtue is knowledge, a trail-blazer for the *Phaedo*'s ethics (68c–69d), and a seminal antecedent of Stoic ethics. Virtue is hypothesized to be good. Everything conventionally counted as good – wealth, health, and even it seems cardinal 'virtues' like justice and courage – is in reality not good in its own right, but derivatively, in so far as its use is guided by wisdom, for if it were instead guided by folly it would be positively harmful. It follows that the only underivatively good thing is wisdom itself, that is, knowledge (its functional equivalent in Plato's usage). This

---

7 For geometry as a necessary basis for ethics, cf. *Gorgias* 507c–508a and *Republic* 7.526c–527c. For the idea that the illustration is deliberately obscure, cf. G. E. R. Lloyd, 'The *Meno* and the mysteries of mathematics', *Phronesis* 37 (1992), 166–83.

conclusion is not definitively proved, but if the argument so far is sound it could be denied only by someone willing also to deny the hypothesis that virtue is good. It is a step towards a definition of virtue, but is limited not only by its hypothetical status but also by a question left unsettled at 89a: whether virtue is the whole of wisdom, or just some part of it.

Teaching, knowledge and true opinion

The final phase of the argument (89a–100b), in which Socrates and Meno are joined by the sinister figure of Anytus, takes an unexpectedly empirical turn. The interim conclusion that virtue is teachable, being the sort of thing, namely knowledge, that is subject to teaching, has left unaddressed the question whether it is in fact ever taught. But Socrates now turns to this latter question, in a way that again echoes his strategy in the earlier *Protagoras*. There, having initially argued that virtue is not teachable on the ground that virtuous men have consistently failed to teach their sons to be virtuous (319d–320b), Socrates moved to the opposed viewpoint by arguing that virtue is knowledge, and therefore is after all teachable (361a–b). Here now in the *Meno* he makes the same switch, but in the reverse direction. Thus, the next major portion of the text (89a–96d) is devoted to an argument which turns out to be anecdotally based. If virtue is teachable, who are its teachers? Certainly not sophists, Anytus insists, and Socrates, despite his ironic pretence of surprise, clearly agrees. Rather, teaching virtue is the proper task of a citizen, Anytus continues. But, he has to admit when quizzed by Socrates, in practice virtuous Athenians do not succeed in teaching virtue to their sons. The ostensible conclusion is that virtue is not transmitted by teaching. But readers will have no difficulty in extracting a Platonic subtext according to which Socrates himself, whether or not he realizes it, is the authentic teacher of virtue. And if he has moved away from his initial conclusion that virtue is knowledge and therefore teachable, that may, at least from an authorial viewpoint, reflect not the falsity of the conclusion but its present status as mere true opinion, which we are about to learn is inherently volatile (cf. 89c–d).

At 96d–98c Socrates introduces a vital new perspective. They have been assuming all along that things are good if and only if they are guided by wisdom, that is, by knowledge. But on reflection it seems that true opinion must produce just the same results. Someone who had merely true opinion about the road to Larisa would be as good a guide to those going there as someone who had travelled it before and therefore knew it. Plato thus opens up the central epistemological question how, if at all, knowledge differs from true opinion, a question destined to play a key role in the *Republic* (476d–480a) and *Theaetetus* (200e–210b).

His answer here in the *Meno* is that true opinion is, so long as one has it, as valuable as knowledge, but tends to slip one's grasp and run away. Knowledge differs from it in being 'tied down', and what ties it down is, in his famous phrase, 'reasoning out the cause' (*aitias logismos*, 98a). 'And this, Meno, my friend,' Socrates adds, 'is recollection, as we have earlier agreed.' The back-reference is to 85c–d, where (see p. xvii) it was multiple and varied repetition of the questioning that was said to turn true opinion into knowledge. Why this latter procedure should be thought equivalent to 'working out the cause' is no easy question. But at any rate the implicit definition, 'Knowledge is true belief bound down by reasoning out the cause', has been judged by many to be Plato's most successful account of knowledge. It is one that deeply influenced Aristotle.

In the final stages of the dialogue (98c–100c) Socrates sifts through the options previously considered. Virtue is not acquired by nature, since it has been shown to be either knowledge or true belief, neither of which is naturally possessed. Nor is it attainable by teaching, since there are no teachers of it. Nor is it in fact knowledge, since if it were it *would* be subject to teaching. The only option left is that virtue, as manifested by those great political figures who failed to teach it to their sons, comes from true opinion, which in its turn, since it is not transmitted by teaching, must be a matter of inspiration. Socrates assumes such inspiration to be divine, but we may take what he has in mind to be, roughly speaking, political instincts. Good politicians, treated here as the paradigm of virtue, have no science or other expertise: they just have a nose for the right decisions.

The final page throws us two thoughts to ponder. First, an authentically virtuous politician, capable of transmitting virtue to others, is still a possibility (100a). Here we inevitably think of Socrates, who in the *Gorgias* (521d) describes himself as the only true politician in Athens, since only he seeks to improve his fellow-citizens. Secondly, the implied slight to existing politicians is likely to anger Anytus, Socrates foresees (100b–c), thus foreshadowing the judicial proceedings against him. With these veiled allusions to Plato's broader *oeuvre*, the conversation ends.

The *Phaedo*

The scene

Socrates, now tried and convicted, sits in his death cell, his execution just hours away. According to the account narrated by Phaedo (himself a Socratic philosopher of some note), Socrates whiles away those final hours explaining to a group of intimate friends why he is facing his own death with such startling equanimity. Uniquely for the Platonic corpus, Plato's absence is expressly noted (59b), perhaps to emphasize that he is not offering us a historical transcript of Socrates' last conversation. Correspondingly, despite its contextualization at a key point in Socrates' biography, the *Phaedo* is widely agreed to belong to Plato's middle period, and to place in Socrates' mouth a two-world metaphysics with no precedent in the early group of dialogues.

The leading interlocutors, Thebans named Simmias and Cebes, are philosophical hybrids: members of the Socratic circle, but also much influenced by the Pythagorean Philolaus. That the soul is immortal, and transmigrates, was the most famous of all Pythagorean doctrines. Yet in the *Phaedo* we encounter two philosophers whose exposure to Pythagoreanism has left them unconvinced of the soul's immortality, so that they have to be persuaded of it instead by Socrates. And in the frame dialogue, in which Phaedo narrates the main conversation to a Pythagorean named Echecrates, the latter confesses to sharing the doubts expressed by Simmias and Cebes (88c–d). This can be interpreted as amounting to an ownership claim on Plato's part: the doctrine of the soul's immortality is more Platonic property than Pythagorean, for it can be proved only with the help of two Platonic discoveries, voiced here by Socrates: the theory of Forms, and the doctrine that all learning is recollection.

The main stages of the narrated conversation are as follows.

Stage 1 (57a–69e): Socrates' defence

The conversation focuses increasingly on the subject of death. Asked by his friends to justify his declaration that a true philosopher is content to die, Socrates offers a 'defence' (63b, 69d–e) of his attitude which he hopes will be more successful than his defence speech at his trial (as recreated by Plato in his *Apology*). The underlying theme is that death is the complete separation of soul from body, and that philosophy, as the process of making the soul function with increasing independence of the body, is properly seen as a step towards this final state. When, first, soul and body are in partnership as they are during a human lifetime, the soul's agenda can easily be infected by that of the body. Desires for bodily satisfaction, and the pursuit of money, war and the like, which serve the same ultimate bodily aims, belong fundamentally to the body. Philosophy teaches the soul to minimize the body's goals and to seek instead its own intrinsic good, wisdom. Thus the first plank of Socrates' defence is asceticism. The second is a newly emphatic anti-empiricism. Philosophy promotes this soul-body severance by enabling the intellect to attain direct access to reality (equated with the Forms, first introduced at 65d–e), not mediated by those seriously misleading instruments of the body, the sense organs.

Plato had always been interested in the parallel treatment of soul and body, but what we are now seeing is a much more radical dualism than that, one in which soul and body become antithetical to each other, and the ideal for the soul is to leave the body behind.

Stage 2 (69e–107b): the proofs of immortality

Socrates' foregoing 'defence' has rested on the assumption that the soul can in fact survive the body – that instead of sharing the body's end it is 'indestructible' and 'immortal'. Socrates is now challenged to prove the truth of this. Simmias and Cebes, although sympathetic to Socrates' view, cannot overcome their irrational fear that upon the demise of the body the soul simply dissipates like smoke. This attempted set of proofs occupies the great bulk of the dialogue. Its landmarks are a series of formal arguments: the Cyclical Argument, the Recollection Argument, the Affinity Argument, and the Final Argument, to all of which we will return below.

Since antiquity these arguments have attracted, often deservedly, a wide range of criticisms. There is a consequent tendency to infer that Plato himself must have regarded them as weak, even fallacious. This would be surprising. The *Phaedo* is Plato's attempted answer to the puzzle why Socrates, to the consternation of his friends, embraced his own death with complete calm. The arguments placed in Socrates' mouth contain Plato's explanation: Socrates had come to understand that death is not annihilation, but the soul's blessed release from bodily confinement and its continued existence in a new state of purity and fulfilment. If Plato had set out to show his master founding this conclusion on faulty arguments, he would have been entirely undermining his long-sustained portrayal of Socrates as a paradigm of the philosophical life.

The important objections raised by Simmias and Cebes (85e–88b) may show that in Plato's eyes the first three arguments are not yet enough to establish the immortality of the soul, but far from suggesting that these arguments are fallacious the two interlocutors treat them as successful in proving the soul's capacity for disembodied existence (e.g. 87a, 92d–e). And neither detects any flaw in the Last Argument, Socrates' proof of absolute immortality, which Cebes indeed regards as conclusive (107a–b).

The ensuing survey of the arguments will therefore try to focus as much on their strengths as on their vulnerabilities. There is no reason to doubt that Plato both believed in the immortality of the soul and regarded these arguments as cumulatively corroborating it.

Stage 3 (107c–115a): the myth

Given the now completed proofs that the soul survives death, Socrates offers to sketch what he thinks death must be like, largely in the form of a myth which draws heavily on existing religious traditions but also innovates daringly. It is founded on a purported revelation about the earth's real shape. It is spherical, and so structured as to have three different atmospheres (as we might call them): water in the lowest regions, air above that, and aether (purer than air) in the upper reaches. The souls of the dead undergo judgement and, where appropriate, punishment in a network of underground rivers and lakes, and are then reincarnated in an atmosphere appropriate to their level of impurity or purity: the least pure in water, some like us in air, and the purest in Olympus-like dwellings up in the aether. The life of the aether-dwellers is described in some detail: they are very long-lived and happy, have direct contact with the gods, etc. Yet other souls, the myth briefly adds, go to even finer abodes, where they are granted permanent disembodiment.

The function of the myths in Plato's dialogues has long been a matter of debate, and the *Phaedo* myth is no exception. Readers will want to make their own judgements on the question. But two hints are in order. First, the pure life of the aether-dwellers can be read as a close approximation to disembodiment, and to that extent as a way of graphically conveying to the reader why total disembodiment is the supremely desirable goal.

Secondly, the myth seems to take up an earlier passage (97b–99c) in which Socrates, describing his youthful flirtation with natural science, reports his subsequent disappointment with the physicist Anaxagoras. The latter had said, promisingly in Socrates' eyes, that everything in the world is caused by intelligence, yet had then failed to show precisely that which one would expect of an intelligently structured world, namely that it is the *best* way for things to be. For example, instead of explaining the earth's shape and position in terms of why that was the best arrangement, Anaxagoras had contented himself with 'assigning the causality to air, aether, water and the like, as well as many other oddities' (98c), items which in reality cannot be causes but just necessary conditions of the cause's successful operation (99a–b). A subtext of the myth is to restore air, water and aether to this latter role, and to sketch how the shape and position of the earth really could, as Socrates had hoped, be explained in terms of why it is best for things to be so – namely, to enable the just progression or demotion of souls between one incarnation and the next.

Stage 4 (115a–118a): the death scene

Socrates' last minutes as he drinks the hemlock, utters his enigmatic last words, and takes his departure, are among the most celebrated in all literature. The contrast between Socrates' calm and the anguish of his companions leaves us with the sense that his levels of understanding and self-mastery are, in the last analysis, of an altogether different order from theirs.

Evaluation of arguments

It is now time to return to some of the dialogue's individual arguments in favour of the soul's immortality. Here one feature in particular deserves stressing at the outset, in further support of the above contention that we should not be too quick to dismiss the arguments as consciously weak. Some of the arguments are less defences of the soul's immortality *ab initio* than attempts to provide formal corroboration of an existing religious tradition. As Socrates has already observed in the *Meno* (81a–c), alluding particularly to the religious movement known as Orphism, one can learn from priests, priestess and poets that the soul survives death and is eventually reincarnated. And that the souls of the dead exist in Hades was a well-entrenched popular belief too, with its roots in Homer (*Odyssey* 11). Socrates' aim in the *Phaedo* is to establish both the scientific respectability and the real meaning of these traditions. The soul's survival in Hades and its eventual reincarnation start out with the credibility that ancient tradition is assumed to confer on a belief, and Socrates' central strategy is to establish scientific laws (as we might call them) to which these particular beliefs conform. Arguments which fail as complete proofs of a thesis may nevertheless have considerable corroborative force when used in this way.

Cyclical Argument (70c–72d)

Socrates' foundation for the Cyclical Argument is a universal theory concerning change, arguably the first in the Western philosophical canon. In any domain (physical, mathematical, moral, etc.), whenever some subject acquires or loses a property which has an opposite, the change is between that pair of opposites: for example, cooling is a transition from hot to cold, or from hotter to colder; falling asleep is a transition from awake to asleep; and separation is a transition from together to apart. Moreover, change between opposites is reciprocal, and proceeds in a cycle. The hot comes from the cold, and vice versa. Likewise the waking come from the sleeping, and vice versa, and the combined comes from the separated, and vice versa.

Another such pair of opposites, Socrates continues, is living and dead. That the dead come from the living is uncontroversially true. We should therefore infer that the living likewise come from the dead. This is taken to mean that at the time of birth a soul is being reincarnated in a body, that at the time of its death it will again leave that body, and so on in an endless cycle.

Critics have exposed a number of weaknesses in this argument. In particular, the correct opposite of alive is probably not 'dead', as assumed here, but something like 'lifeless', a term which avoids the implication that new life must come from individuals who first had, then lost, a previous life. But note at least that much here depends on one's definition of 'dead'. For Socrates and his interlocutors (64c, 67d), life is the conjunction of soul and body, death their separation. The first two examples of reciprocal processes quoted above (the cyclical interchange of heating/cooling, and waking/falling asleep) already provided a beguiling analogue for a cyclical interchange between coming to life and dying, but in the light of Socrates' definition of death we can see that the third pair, combination/separation, is even more artfully chosen. From the body's point of view, the life-death interchange corresponds to a heating-cooling cycle; from the soul's point of view, it closely mimics the waking-sleeping cycle; and from their common point of view, it is a special case of the combination-separation cycle.

Recollection Argument (72e–77a)

This is among Plato's most celebrated, and controversial, arguments. Building on the defence of Recollection in the *Meno* (see pp. xvii–xix), it purports to provide additional proof that the soul must have pre-existed the body, since the soul brings to this life concealed knowledge which it can only have acquired beforehand. This conclusion, when combined with that of the Cyclical Argument, will be taken to show (77c–d) that the soul must also continue to exist after leaving the body.

An additional consequence is that during its discarnate phases the soul must possess wisdom (76c). This answers Cebes' earlier request that the disembodied soul should be shown not only to survive but also to have some 'power and wisdom' (70b). It thereby implicitly wards off the threat posed by Homer's description of departed souls, 'the dead who have no understanding' (*Odyssey* 11.475–6), and vindicates Socrates' reinterpretation of the tradition so as to make death a positive advance.

The bare bones of the argument are as follows.

(A) If certain conditions are fulfilled, a cognitive act counts as a case of 'recollection' or 'being reminded' (the Greek verb *anamimnēskesthai*, along with its cognate noun *anamnēsis*, combines both senses) (73c–74a).

(B) There is a familiar cognitive act by which, as a result of seeing sensible equal things, one comes to think of the Form of Equal (74a–c).

(C) This cognitive act, since it exactly matches the conditions for recollection in (A), is a case of recollection (74c–d).

(D) Therefore, since you can recollect only what you previously knew (73c), the Form of Equal was known to us prior to that cognitive act (74d–75a).

(E) The knowledge of it was not acquired at any time between birth and the cognitive act (75a–76c).

(F) Nor can it have been acquired at the moment of birth (76c–d).

(G) Therefore it was acquired before birth (76c).

(H) Therefore our souls existed before our birth, and possessed wisdom (76c).

Much of the controversy focuses on (A) and (B). (A) offers various examples of being reminded. The relationship of x to y in virtue of which perceiving x reminds you of y may be, for instance, that of being owned by y, being a friend of y, or resembling y. But the special case on which Socrates then focuses, the resemblance relation, is picked out because of its detailed correspondence to the cognitive act described in (B). When you see a portrait of Simmias, (i) it may prompt you to recall Simmias himself, whom you previously knew, and (ii) you cannot help thinking about how accurate a likeness it is. Correspondingly, when you see a pair of sticks equal in length, (i) it may prompt you to think of the Equal itself, and (ii) you cannot help being aware of their deficient likeness to that Form. As Simmias himself is to his portrait, so implicitly is the Form of Equal to sensible instances of equality: a paradigm towards which they are striving, but achieving only a deficient resemblance.

In what, then, does this deficiency consist? The question is of great importance to our reading of the Recollection Argument. Some have thought in addition that its answer holds the key to Plato's thesis (e.g. *Republic* 479a–b) of the 'compresence of opposites', according to which no sensible particular manifests one of a pair of opposites without also manifesting the other. However, not only is no such universal thesis yet visible in the *Phaedo*, but the Last Argument (see below) explicitly draws attention to sensible particulars that contravene it (e.g. fire is only hot and in no way cold, and snow the converse). The present argument cannot safely be assumed to apply to all predicates, or even to all opposites.

'Equal' functions for Plato as a size relation (rather than, e.g., a numerical one), intermediate between large and small. All three terms are ones he regards as easily grasped and defined, and that may be why Simmias readily agrees the Form of Equal to be already known to 'us' (74b), whether that be everybody or, at any rate, all those present. Those like Simmias who know the Equal itself can testify that it is not subject to a conflict of appearances such that it might appear to be unequal (or, perhaps, Unequal). Yet the equivalent confusion can and does occur with regard to the equality of sticks or stones: they *can* also appear unequal. Just how they can do so is a matter of huge textual debate at 74b: 'Don't equal stones and sticks sometimes, despite being the same ones, appear at one time equal, at another not?' Most English editors and translators have preferred the variant reading 'appear equal to one but not to another', and have been divided as to whether to construe it as 'appear . . . to' or 'equal to'. The latter is the less likely, since the sticks' and stones' equality seemed to be equality *to each other* when they were first introduced as ones that simply 'were equal' (74b). Moreover, in this same description the sticks and stones are assumed to be actually equal, and not also unequal. The deficiency to which Socrates draws attention lies not in their possessing inequality as well, but in their ability to *appear* to do so. It is that capacity for misleading appearance that distinguishes them from the corresponding Form, an object of pure thought which is grasped either just as it is or not at all.

What, finally, is the cognitive act by which a Form is recollected? This again has generated much controversy. It has often been supposed that Plato is explaining what rational thought itself is, or at any rate how we are able to use *a priori* concepts: you cannot, for example, entertain the thought 'These sticks are equal' without drawing to some extent on your innate grasp of what Equality (the Form of Equal) is. On this view, everybody is in the process of recollecting most of the time, although only those who go on to investigate and define the Forms in question *fully* recollect them. At the other extreme, it has been proposed that recollection is done only by a privileged few, namely philosophers, to whom alone the 'we' at 74a–b refers.

Arguably the former interpretation, for all its philosophical attractions, pays too little attention to the specification, repeated from the *Meno*, that it is 'those who learn' (75e, 76a) who recollect. And the latter, more restrictive interpretation, has its own disadvantage too: it risks undermining the argument's aim (amply borne out by the myth) of showing that *all* souls, not just those of philosophers, have a discarnate existence. An intermediate position not without merits is to suppose that very much the same constituency is envisaged as in the *Meno*. Anybody, even a slave, can learn (that is, successfully study disciplines like geometry) and it is only when they do so that they start to recollect. Examining a figure formed out of equal sticks, and thereby thinking about the properties of equality as such, might be one way of starting off this learning process.

Affinity Argument (78b–80b)

Although this next argument concludes that soul is such as to be 'altogether incapable of being disintegrated, or nearly so' (80b), it is a very different kind of argument from the two that precede it. It is designed to assuage irrational fears that remain despite the force of those formal demonstrations, and does so by arguing that, given a Platonic bipartition of reality into physical body and intelligible Forms, soul has far more in common with the latter than with the former, and might therefore very reasonably be expected to share the Forms' indestructibility. In a way, the argument's most significant function is to ground what follows it (80c–84b). There Socrates professes his confidence that a philosopher's soul will, after death, gravitate to its natural environment, the realm of Forms, whereas that of a non-philosopher, with its bodily leanings, will yearn for reincarnation.

Last Argument (96a–107b)

The Affinity Argument concluded that the soul is 'altogether incapable of being disintegrated, or nearly so' (80b). Socrates' cautious wording here served to prompt a nagging doubt in Cebes, which finally surfaces at 86e–88b: might a soul not outlive a whole series of incarnations, yet itself perish in the end? The first part of Socrates' answer to this is a classic autobiographical account of his evolving views on causation (cf. pp. xxv–xxvi on the myth), according to which he ended up resorting to the principle that Forms are causes. The passage has potentially deep implications for Socrates', and more especially Plato's, intellectual development, but its relation to the final phase of the argument is far from clear, and we will bypass it here. The real finale is 102a–107b. Its interpretation is massively disputed, so the following account should be taken as no more than one way of reading it.

Nominating the Form of F as the cause of things being F (for example, Beauty as the cause of things being beautiful) has been seen to be 'safe', in that it never generates contradictions, but also 'simple-minded', in the sense of 'uninformative' (100c–e). In this final phase Socrates introduces a new kind of cause, one which is on the one hand still 'safe', but on the other 'ingenious' where the old kind was 'simple-minded'. For example, instead of saying simple-mindedly that 'heat' makes things hot, we can say that fire makes things hot. Fire itself is inalienably hot, and cannot take on the opposite property, cold. Whatever fire is present in, it imports heat to that thing. Likewise, snow is inalienably cold, and whatever it occupies it makes cold. Nor is this class limited to physical stuffs, since another set of its members is the numbers. For example, the number three (not the Form of three, but a particular instance of tripleness) is numerically odd, and whatever it characterizes it makes likewise odd.

A member of this heterogeneous class can be described as follows. For some value of F, whose opposite is G, the item in question is a particular which (1) is essentially F; (2) imports F-ness to whatever it occupies; and (3) is incapable of taking on G-ness. On the approach of G-ness, this entity must either *retreat* or *perish*. We will here illustrate the description with just the simplest case, snow. Snow (1) is essentially cold; (2) whatever it occupies it makes cold; and (3) it is incapable of becoming hot (that is, there could not be hot snow). When heat approaches snow, the snow must either retreat, i.e. get out of its way, or perish, i.e. melt. Something equivalent must apply to fire in relation to heat, and to the number three in relation to oddness, even though in this last case the meanings of 'retreat' and 'perish' will have to be reinterpreted appropriately. (A guess: my three pairs of shoes are numerically odd; when I count them as six shoes, their oddness retreats; when I burn one pair, it perishes.) Despite such complications, the heterogeneity of the class is vital to Socrates' argument. For it is now to be applied to a soul, something easily thought of as ontologically unique. To forestall the objection that soul may not sufficiently be analogous to snow, or to fire, Socrates has introduced a universal principle, entirely neutral as regards domain.

The main proof now ensues at 105c–d. Another member of the same class is soul: it always imports life to what it occupies, and is itself incapable of being dead. This is already enough to show that it is 'deathless' or 'immortal' (105e), in the strong sense that its death is as impossible as three's being an even number.

It is widely doubted by scholars that this is anything more than an interim step in the argument, on the dubious ground that Plato still has to infer from it that soul is imperishable. But since soul is essentially alive, there is no way that it could perish other than by dying, and the extra step is not needed. One might support the argument by pointing out that whatever x dies is thereafter a dead x: for example, Plato is a dead philosopher. So if a soul died it would have to be thereafter a dead soul – something as impossible as an even trio or a hot snowball.

What then is the point of the argument's continuation at 105e–107a, where soul's imperishability *is* inferred from its immortality? It is to establish a strictly supplementary point, one that at last puts to work the 'retreat or perish' principle. Leaving aside soul, any other member of this class, when approached by the property opposite to the one it essentially bears, has the twin options of (a) retreating and (b) perishing, but emphatically it cannot (c) stay and take on that opposite property. For instance, the snowball can (a) retreat from the heat or (b) stay and melt, but cannot (c) stay and become a hot snowball. Soul, however, is a special exception. If upon the approach of death it were (b) to perish, it would also (c) take on the opposite property to the one it bears, that is, become a dead soul. Therefore in the special case of soul, perishing is ruled out, and on the approach of death there is only one thing left for it to do: it retreats. The meaning of 'retreat' has been left flexible, but in this concluding moment Socrates and his companions are in no doubt as to what it amounts to: soul must leave the body and go to Hades (106e–107a). Thus, at the very close of the defence of immortality, at the point where argument reaches its limit, and is about to give way to eschatological myth, Socrates is seen yet again reaffirming the Hades mythology.

Other highlights

Further motifs barely touched on in the above synopsis include: the curious interrelation of pleasure and pain (60a–c); the veto on suicide (62a–e); the analysis of virtue in terms of wisdom alone (68c–69d; cf. *Meno* 87d–89a); the transmigration of inferior souls into appropriate life forms (81e–82b); Socrates' swansong (84d–85b); the proposal, and subsequent refutation by Socrates, of the theory that soul is an 'attunement' of the bodily elements rather than an independently existing entity (85e–86d, 92a–95b); the critique of causal theories (96a–101c); the method of hypothesis (99e–102a; cf. *Meno* 86d–87d); and the theory of immanent forms, such as 'the largeness in us' (102b–103c).

Epilogue

From the cocoon of Socrates' legacy we have now seen a mature and independent philosophy emerge. The *Meno* foreshadows or outlines, and the *Phaedo* proceeds to develop, such bold doctrines as those of immortality, Recollection and the Forms. Thereafter these continue to feature, severally or collectively, in major Platonic dialogues conventionally dated after the *Phaedo*, notably the *Republic*, *Phaedrus* and *Timaeus*.

In reading our two dialogues, we are witnessing nothing less than the arrival of Platonism itself.

Chronology

BC

399	Trial and execution of Socrates; dramatic date of *Phaedo*
mid-380s	Plato's first visit to Sicily, and contact with Pythagoreans; Philolaus dies
c. 380s	*Meno* written; Gorgias dies; Plato founds the Academy at Athens
c. 370s	*Phaedo* written
c. 366	Plato's second visit to Sicily; Aristotle becomes student at Academy
361	Plato's third visit to Sicily
347	Plato dies

Further reading

In preparing the translations we have followed the latest Oxford Classical Text of Plato, *Platonis Opera*, except where indicated in the notes. The relevant volumes are: for the *Meno*, vol. 3 (J. Burnet (ed.), Oxford, 1903); for the *Phaedo*, vol. 1 (E.A. Duke *et al.* (ed.), Oxford, 1995). In the latter volume, the editor of the *Phaedo* itself is J. C. G. Strachan.

Further discussion of the Greek texts can be found in W. J. Verdenius, 'Notes on Plato's *Phaedo*', *Mnemosyne* 4.11 (1958), 193–243; R. S. Bluck, *Plato's Meno* (Cambridge, 1961); R. W. Sharples, *Plato: Meno* (Warminster, 1985); J. Burnet, *Plato's Phaedo* (Oxford, 1911); and Christopher Rowe, *Plato: Phaedo* (Cambridge, 1993).

Bluck, Sharples, Burnet and Rowe also provide detailed discussion of the Greek wording and so are valuable resources for those who wish to read the dialogues in the original language. For further philosophical commentary consult David Gallop, *Plato: Phaedo* (Oxford, 1975), whose thorough notes and commentary remain essential reading for advanced study of the *Phaedo*. Rowe's meticulous commentary has been a constant support during the preparation of this volume, and we have taken up many of its suggestions without separate acknowledgement. Important commentaries in other European languages include Monique Dixsaut, *Platon, Phédon* (Paris, 1991); Dorothea Frede, *Platons 'Phaidon'. Der Traum von der Unsterblichkeit der Seele* (Darmstadt, 1999); and the especially innovative Theodor Ebert, *Platon, Phaidon* (Göttingen, 2004).

There are now several book-length discussions of the *Meno*, such as the excellent monograph by Dominic Scott, *Plato's Meno* (Cambridge, 2006). See also Jane Day, *Plato's Meno in Focus* (London, 1994), which provides a translation, an introduction and a collection of essays, and

Roslyn Weiss, *Virtue in the Cave: Moral Inquiry in Plato's Meno* (Oxford, 2001). There has been much debate about the importance of definition in the *Meno* and in other dialogues. For the start of the controversy see P. T. Geach, 'Plato's *Euthyphro*: an analysis and commentary', *Monist* 50 (1966), 369–82; for a more recent account see Charles Kahn, *Plato and the Socratic Dialogue: The Philosophical Use of a Literary Form* (Cambridge, 1996), ch. 6.

Books that discuss epistemology in the *Meno* are in several cases important reading for the *Phaedo* too. Dominic Scott, *Recollection and Experience: Plato's Theory of Learning and its Successors* (Cambridge, 1995) is a ground-breaking account of recollection in both dialogues. Gail Fine, *Plato on Knowledge and Forms* (Oxford, 2003) contains key essays on Forms in the *Phaedo* as well as on epistemology in the *Meno* (on which see also her 'Knowledge and true belief in the *Meno*', *Oxford Studies in Ancient Philosophy* 27 (2004), 41–81). Russell Dancy, *Plato's Introduction of Forms* (Cambridge, 2004) discusses some central themes of both dialogues: definition, recollection and hypothesis in the *Meno*, and Forms in the *Phaedo*.

Much has been written about the arguments for immortality in the *Phaedo*. A good place to start is David Bostock, *Plato's Phaedo* (Oxford, 1986), which provides clear analysis of all these arguments. For an account of the overall argumentative structure of the *Phaedo* see Michael Pakaluk, 'Degrees of separation in the *Phaedo*', *Phronesis* 48 (2003), 89–115. Those interested in the argument from recollection will still benefit from the classic account in J. L. Ackrill, *Essays on Plato and Aristotle* (Oxford, 1997), ch. 1. See also Scott, *Recollection and Experience*, and, for defence of the interpretation outlined in the Introduction and of the text used in our translation, David Sedley, 'Form-particular resemblance in Plato's *Phaedo*', *Proceedings of the Aristotelian Society* 106.3 (2006), 311–27, and 'Equal sticks and stones' in Dominic Scott (ed.), *Maieusis: Essays in Ancient Philosophy in Honour of Myles Burnyeat* (Oxford, 2007), 68–86.

There is a huge literature on the various parts of Socrates' elaborate response to Cebes in *Phaedo* 95e–107b. For the method of hypothesis see D. T. J. Bailey, 'Logic and music in Plato's *Phaedo*', *Phronesis* 50.2 (2005), 95–115; for causation see David Sedley, 'Platonic causes', *Phronesis* 43.2 (1998), 114–32. For Socrates' Last Argument at 102a–107b consult Dorothea Frede, 'The final proof of the immortality of the soul in Plato's *Phaedo* 102a–107a', *Phronesis* 23.1 (1978), 27–41, and Nicholas Denyer,

'The *Phaedo*'s final argument', in Scott, *Maievsis: Essays in Ancient Philosophy*, 87–96.

Two monographs discuss drama and myth as well as argument in the *Phaedo*: Kenneth Dorter, *Plato's Phaedo: An Interpretation* (Toronto, 1982), and Ronna Burger, *The Phaedo: A Platonic Labyrinth* (New Haven, 1984). The *Phaedo*'s myth is discussed in David Sedley, 'Teleology and myth in the *Phaedo*', *Proceedings of the Boston Area Colloquium in Ancient Philosophy* 5 (1990), 359–83; Peter Kingsley, *Ancient Philosophy, Mystery, and Magic* (Oxford, 1995); Gabor Betegh, 'Tale, theology and teleology in the *Phaedo*' in Catalin Partenie (ed.), *Plato's Myths* (Cambridge, 2009), 77–100; and Kathryn A. Morgan, *Myth and Philosophy from the Presocratics to Plato* (Cambridge, 2000). See also Diskin Clay, 'The art of Glaukos', *American Journal of Philology* 106 (1985), 230–6.

There has been much speculation on the meaning of Socrates' last words in the *Phaedo*, including Glenn Most, 'A cock for Asclepius', *Classical Quarterly* 43 (1993), 96–111.

The themes of the *Meno* and of the *Phaedo* recur often in other Platonic dialogues. Those who wish to examine these further passages can start with Tim Chappell, *The Plato Reader* (Edinburgh, 1996), which contains in English translation some of Plato's most important discussions of definition, virtue, soul, knowledge and Forms. For fuller comparisons consult the translations in John M. Cooper (ed.), *Plato, Complete Works* (Indianapolis, 1997). There Cooper also provides a general introduction to interpreting and studying Plato, for which see also Christopher Rowe, 'Plato' in David Sedley (ed.), *The Cambridge Companion to Greek and Roman Philosophy* (Cambridge, 2003), 98–124, or Richard Kraut, 'Introduction to the study of Plato' in Richard Kraut (ed.), *The Cambridge Companion to Plato* (Cambridge, 1992), 1–50.

For information on the characters of the dialogues, and also the problem of Plato's precise year of birth, see Debra Nails, *The People of Plato: A Prosopography of Plato and Other Socratics* (Indianapolis, 2002).

Translator's note

As explained at p. xxxvii, the translations follow the current edition of the Oxford Classical Text (OCT) of Plato except where otherwise indicated. The indications of departure from the OCT are included in the footnotes to the translations. Where the content of a footnote is purely of this textual kind and does not bear on interpretative issues, the footnote marker is accompanied by an asterisk.

Meno

MENO:[1] Can you tell me, Socrates, whether virtue is teachable?[2] Or is 70a
it not teachable, but attainable by practice? Or is it attainable neither by
practice nor by learning, and do people instead acquire it by nature, or in
some other way?

SOCRATES:[3] In the past, Meno, the Thessalians were renowned among
the Greeks and admired for both horsemanship and wealth, but now, I 70b
think, they are admired for wisdom as well, and particularly the fellow-
citizens of your friend Aristippus, the men of Larisa. You have Gorgias[4]
to thank for this, for since he came to that city he has made the leading
Aleuadae,[5] of whom your lover Aristippus is one, court him for his
wisdom, as well as the leading people among the other Thessalians. And
besides he has given you this very habit of fearlessly and magnificently
answering any question anyone asks, as is only reasonable for people who
have knowledge, since he himself makes himself available for any Greek 70c
who wishes to pose him any question he likes, and answers absolutely
everyone.

But the situation here, my dear Meno, is quite the opposite: there has
been a drought of wisdom, as it were, and in all likelihood wisdom has 71a
vanished from these parts and migrated to your people. At any rate, if
you want to put a question like that to one of the people here, any one of

---

Footnotes marked with an asterisk indicate departures from the Oxford Classical Text and do not
discuss the translation or interpretation of the dialogues.

[1] On Meno, see p. xii.   [2] On the word translated 'teachable', see p. xii n. 1.
[3] On Socrates, see p. ix.
[4] Gorgias of Leontini (c. 485–c. 380 BC), a leading sophist and rhetorician, featured extensively in
the first part of Plato's *Gorgias*.
[5] The ruling family of Larisa, in Thessaly.

them will laugh and say: 'Stranger, you must think I am richly blessed, at least if you expect me to know whether virtue is teachable or how people come to have it. I am so far from knowing whether or not it's teachable that even the very question *what on earth virtue is* is one regarding which I don't in fact have any knowledge at all.'

71b   Now that is true of me as well, Meno. I share my fellow-citizens' poverty in this matter, and reproach myself for knowing nothing at all about virtue. But how could I know what *sort* of thing something is, when I don't know *what* it is? Or do you think that, if someone doesn't know at all who Meno is, it is possible for him to know whether Meno is beautiful or rich or even of good birth, or, as it may be, the opposites of these? Do you think that possible?

71c   MENO: No. But do you really not know even what virtue is, Socrates, and is that the news about you we are to take back home as well?

SOCRATES: Yes, and not only that, my friend, but also that I don't think I've yet even met anyone else who knows.

MENO: What? Didn't you meet Gorgias when he was here?

SOCRATES: I did.

MENO: And so you didn't think that he knew?

SOCRATES: My memory isn't great, Meno, so I can't say now how he struck me back then. Perhaps, however, he does know, and perhaps you

71d know what he said. So remind me what he said. Or, if you want, tell me yourself. For I presume you agree with him.

MENO: I do.

SOCRATES: Then let's forget about him, since he isn't here anyway. But as for you, by the gods, Meno, what do you say virtue is? Tell me and don't keep it to yourself, so that, if you and Gorgias prove to know, my mistake when I claimed never yet to have met someone who knew may turn out to be a most fortunate one.

71e   MENO: Well, it isn't difficult to say, Socrates. First, if you want to take the virtue of a man, it is easy to state that the virtue of a man is to be competent at managing the affairs of his city, and in so doing to benefit friends and harm enemies, and to take care that nothing of the latter kind befalls him himself. Then if you want the virtue of a woman, it isn't hard to explain that she must run her household well, conserving its property and being obedient to her husband. And there is a different virtue for a child – one for a female child, one for a male – and one for an older man,

who may be a freeman if you like, or a slave if you like. There are also 72a
very many other virtues. And so there is no puzzle in saying what virtue
is. For each of us, you see, and for each pursuit, there is the relevant
virtue to match each activity and age. And I think the same is true of the
relevant vice, Socrates.

SOCRATES: I seem to have met with a great piece of good fortune,
Meno, if in seeking one virtue I have discovered that you have a whole
swarm of virtues at your disposal. But, Meno, with regard to this image
of 'swarms', suppose I asked you about just what it is to be a bee,[6] and 72b
you said that there were many kinds of bees. What answer would you
give me if I asked you: 'Do you say that it is their being bees that makes
them of many different kinds? Or do they not differ at all because of this,
but because of something else, such as beauty or largeness or something
else of that kind?' Tell me, how would you answer if you were asked this
question?

MENO: Like this: in so far as they are bees, one bee doesn't differ at all
from another.

SOCRATES: Now suppose I said to you next: 'Then tell me about 72c
precisely that, Meno: what do you say it is that makes them all no different,
but the same?' You would have an answer for me, I take it?

MENO: I would.

SOCRATES: Likewise then when it comes to the virtues too – even if
they are of many kinds, they still all have one and the same form[7] because
of which they are virtues. And when responding to questions it is right,
presumably, to look to this form before explaining what virtue really is to
the person who asked the question. Or do you not get my point? 72d

MENO: Well, I *think* I do. But I don't yet grasp what you're asking, at
least as I would like to.

SOCRATES: Do you think that it is true only of virtue, Meno, that
there is a different one for a man, a different one for a woman, and so on?
Or do you regard health and largeness and strength in the same way? Do
you believe that there is a different health for a man, a different one for

---

[6] 'what it is to be . . .': the Greek word is *ousia*, 'being', the abstract noun from the verb 'be'. It can also be translated 'essence', and it comes to be associated especially with the transcendent Forms, cf. *Phaedo* 65d, 76d, etc.
[7] The Greek word *eidos* here comes to be one of Plato's favourites for his theory of transcendent 'Forms'.

a woman? Or is the form the same everywhere, provided that it is health,
72e whether in a man or in anyone else?

MENO: Health, at least, is I think the same both for a man and for a woman.

SOCRATES: Largeness and strength as well? If a woman is strong, will she be strong because of the same form and the same strength? What I mean by 'the same' is that strength does not differ at all with regard to its being strength depending on whether it is in a man or in a woman. Or do you believe that it does?

MENO: No, I don't.

73a SOCRATES: Whereas virtue *will* differ with regard to its being virtue depending on whether it is in a child or in an elderly person, in a woman or in a man?

MENO: Somehow I think, Socrates, that this case isn't like those other ones.

SOCRATES: Well, weren't you claiming that a man's virtue is to manage a city well, a woman's virtue to manage a house well?

MENO: Yes.

SOCRATES: Now is it possible to manage a city, a house or anything else in a good way, if one doesn't do so in a temperate and just way?

MENO: No, surely not.

73b SOCRATES: If, then, they manage justly and temperately, they will do so because of justice and temperance?

MENO: Necessarily.

SOCRATES: Therefore both the woman and the man need the same things if they are to be good: justice and temperance.

MENO: Yes, they seem to.

SOCRATES: How about a child and an elderly person? Could they ever become good if they were intemperate and unjust?

MENO: Certainly not.

SOCRATES: But they could do so if they were temperate and just?

73c MENO: Yes.

SOCRATES: Then all humans are good in the same way. For they become good by attaining the same things.

MENO: It looks that way.

SOCRATES: And they wouldn't be good in the same way, I presume, if their virtue were not the same.

MENO: Definitely not.

SOCRATES: So since they all have the same virtue, try to say and recall what Gorgias says it is – and you with him.

MENO: The ability to rule over people – what else? Assuming, that is, that you're seeking one thing covering all cases. 73d

SOCRATES: I certainly am. But does a child also have the same virtue, Meno, and does a slave, namely the ability to rule their master? Do you think that one would still be a slave with such authority?

MENO: Not at all, Socrates.

SOCRATES: Right – it's implausible, my friend. Besides, consider this further point. You say that virtue is 'to be able to rule'. Won't we add to that 'justly, and not unjustly'?

MENO: I think so, because justice is virtue, Socrates.

SOCRATES: Virtue, Meno, or *a* virtue? 73e

MENO: What do you mean by that?

SOCRATES: Just what I would say about anything else. For example, if you like, I would say that roundness is a shape, not simply that it is shape.[8] And my reason for describing it like this would be that there are other shapes as well.

MENO: Yes, you'd be right to say that, since I myself say that justice isn't the only virtue, but that there are other virtues as well.

SOCRATES: What are they? Tell me. I would tell you other shapes too, 74a if you asked – so you tell me other virtues.

MENO: Well then, courage seems to me to be a virtue,[9] as do temperance, wisdom, magnificence, and a great many others.

SOCRATES: The very same thing has happened to us again, Meno. Once more we have found many virtues when seeking one, though in a different way from just now. But we can't discover the one virtue which extends through all these.

MENO: That is because I can't yet find one virtue covering all cases in 74b the way you're seeking, Socrates, as I can in the other examples.

SOCRATES: Yes, understandably. But I'll strive to bring us closer,[*10] if I can. You appreciate, I presume, that the following is true in every case. Suppose that someone were to ask you what I just asked, 'What is shape, Meno?', and you replied 'Roundness'. Then suppose that he said

---

[8] For the translation of *schēma* as 'shape', see p. xiv n. 3.
[9] Meno's reply could be translated 'virtue' or 'a virtue'.   [*10] Reading προσβιβάσαι at 74b3.

to you what I said: 'Is roundness shape, or *a* shape?'. Presumably you would reply that it's a shape.

MENO: Certainly.

74c   SOCRATES: Your reason being that there are other shapes as well?

MENO: Yes.

SOCRATES: Right, and if he proceeded to ask you what other sorts of shape there are, you would tell him?

MENO: I would.

SOCRATES: Again, suppose that, along the same lines, he asked you what colour is, you replied 'White', and your questioner then retorted: 'Is white colour, or a colour?'. You would say that it's a colour, because there are others too?

MENO: I would.

SOCRATES: Yes, and if he asked you to mention other colours, you

74d   would tell him others which are no less colours than white is?

MENO: Yes.

SOCRATES: Now imagine that, like me, he pursued the argument and said: 'We keep ending up with a multitude. Don't give me that sort of reply, but since you call this multitude by a certain single name, and say that none of them isn't a shape, despite the fact that they're actually opposite to one another, tell me what this thing is which encompasses the

74e   round no less than the straight, the thing you name shape, saying that the round is no more a shape than the straight is?' Or don't you claim that?

MENO: I do.

SOCRATES: Then when you make such a claim, do you mean to say that the round is no more round than straight, and the straight no more straight than round?

MENO: Certainly not, Socrates.

SOCRATES: And yet you do say that the round is no more shape, at least, than the straight is, nor vice versa.

MENO: True.

75a   SOCRATES: So what on earth is this thing named 'shape'? Try to tell me. Now imagine that you said to the person who was questioning you in this way, either about shape or about colour: 'Look here – I don't even understand what you want, and I don't know what you mean either.' Perhaps he would be taken aback and say: 'Don't you understand that I'm seeking what is the same in all these cases?' Or would you have no answer even in the case of these things, Meno, if someone were to ask you: 'What is the same in the case of all these things, the round and the straight and the other things you call shapes?' Try to say, so that you may then get some practice for your answer about virtue.

MENO: No – you say, Socrates.   75b

SOCRATES: You want me to indulge you?

MENO: Absolutely.

SOCRATES: So will you likewise be willing to tell me about virtue?

MENO: Yes.

SOCRATES: Then I must do my best – because it's worth my while.

MENO: Certainly.

SOCRATES: Right then, let's try to tell you what shape is. Now consider whether you accept this account of what it is: let us take shape to be that which, alone of all things, always accompanies colour. Do you find that sufficient, or do you ask for a different kind of answer? For my part, you see, I would be satisfied even if the account of virtue you gave me were   75c
of this kind.

MENO: But that's simple-minded, Socrates.

SOCRATES: What do you mean?

MENO: I mean that on your account, as I understand it, shape is what always accompanies colour. Maybe so, but if someone were to say that he didn't know colour, and was puzzled about it in the same way as about shape, what do you think your answer would be?

SOCRATES: The truth. And if the questioner were one of the experts in eristic and competitive debate I would tell him: 'That's what I have to   75d
say. But if what I'm saying is incorrect, it's your job to hold me to account and refute it.' If, however, like you and me now, they were friends and wished to have a genuine dialogue with one another, they should find a gentler and more dialectical way to answer. And I suggest that the more dialectical manner is to reply not only with the truth, but in addition through things which the person questioned[11] also admits he knows. So I too will endeavour to speak to you in that way. Tell me: do you use the   75e
term 'end' of something? In the sense of limit and extremity, that is – I mean the same thing by all of these. Perhaps Prodicus would disagree with

---

[11] This is often emended so as to read 'the questioner'. But as the present passage illustrates, in dialectic the respective roles of questioner and answerer can switch at any time. What matters is that either party, if asked, will admit to knowing the thing in question.

us, but I would guess that you, at any rate, describe something as being limited *and* ended.[12] That is what I mean to say, nothing complicated.

MENO: But of course I use those descriptions, and I think I understand your point.

76a   SOCRATES: Very well. Do you describe something as 'surface', and something else as 'solid', such as the ones in geometrical studies?

MENO: I do.

SOCRATES: Now already with these you might understand what I say shape is. For all shape, I say that shape is that at which the solid is limited. Drawing that together I would say that shape is the limit of a solid.

MENO: But what do you say colour is, Socrates?

SOCRATES: Outrageous behaviour, Meno! You set problems for an
76b   old man to answer, but you're not willing yourself to recollect and tell me what on earth Gorgias says virtue is.

MENO: Well, when you answer that question of mine, Socrates, I'll answer you.

SOCRATES: Even if someone had his head covered, Meno, he could tell from your conversation that you're beautiful and still have lovers.

MENO: How?

SOCRATES: Because you do nothing but give orders in the discussion, precisely what fêted boys do, for they play the tyrant as long as they have
76c   the attractions of youth. And at the same time you've probably realised that I'm at the mercy of beauties. So I'll indulge you and answer.

MENO: Yes, indulge me you must.

SOCRATES: Now do you want me to answer you in the style of Gorgias, in the way you would follow best?

MENO: I do, naturally.

SOCRATES: Then do you and he say that things have certain effluences, as Empedocles[13] claims?

MENO: Quite so.

SOCRATES: And that there are channels into which and through which the effluences are conveyed?

MENO: Absolutely.

---

[12] In Plato's dialogues the sophist Prodicus' trademark is to deny that any two words are exact synonyms.

[13] Mid-fifth-century Sicilian philosopher-poet, for whose physical analyses of perception cf. Theophrastus, *On the Senses* 7–11.

SOCRATES: And that some of the effluences fit some of the channels, 76d
but others are too small or large?

MENO: That's true.

SOCRATES: Is there also something you describe as 'sight'?

MENO: Yes.

SOCRATES: Then from this 'mark what I tell thee', as Pindar put it:
colour is effluence of shapes, commensurate with sight and thus perceptible.

MENO: I think that is a superb answer, Socrates.

SOCRATES: Quite, for perhaps such an answer is familiar to you. And
at the same time you realize, I think, that from it you could also say what
sound is, and smell and many other such things. 76e

MENO: Certainly.

SOCRATES: Yes, the answer belongs in a tragedy, Meno. That is why
it pleases you more than the one about shape.

MENO: It does.

SOCRATES: But the better answer isn't this one, son of Alexidemus,
or so I have convinced myself, but the other one. And I imagine that you
wouldn't think so either, if you didn't need, as you said yesterday, to
leave before the mysteries, but were to stay and be initiated.

MENO: But I would stay, Socrates, if you were to tell me many things 77a
of that kind.

SOCRATES: Well, if I do I won't be at all lacking in eagerness, both for
your sake and for mine, although I suspect that I won't be able to tell you
many things like that. But come on, *you* try to keep your promise to *me*:
say what virtue is as a whole and stop making many from one, as jokers
are always saying when people smash something. But leave virtue whole
and intact, and say what it is. I've given you the models, after all. 77b

MENO: Very well, Socrates, I think virtue is, as the poet says, 'to rejoice
in the noble and be proficient'. And I say that this is virtue: to desire noble
things and be proficient at securing them.

SOCRATES: Would you say that the person who desires noble things
desires good things?

MENO: Very much so.

SOCRATES: On the assumption that there are some people who desire
bad things, others who desire good things? Do you not think, my friend, 77c
that everyone desires good things?

MENO: No, I don't.

SOCRATES: But that some people desire bad things?

MENO: Yes.

SOCRATES: Thinking that the bad things are good, do you mean? Or do they actually know that the things are bad, but nonetheless desire them?

MENO: Both happen, I think.

SOCRATES: Do you really think, Meno, that there is anyone who knows that the bad things are bad but nonetheless desires them?

MENO: Certainly.

SOCRATES: What do you mean that he desires? To acquire them?

MENO: Yes, what else?

77d SOCRATES: In the belief that bad things benefit whoever acquires them, or in the knowledge that bad things harm whoever possesses them?

MENO: There are some who do so in the belief that bad things benefit, but others as well who do so in the knowledge that they harm.

SOCRATES: And do you think that those who believe that bad things benefit know that the bad things are bad?

MENO: That I *don't* believe.

SOCRATES: Then it is clear that these people, at least, don't desire bad

77e things, ignorant as they are about them, but desire things they thought were good, but in fact are bad. And so the people who are ignorant about these things and think they are good clearly desire good things. Or don't they?

MENO: These people, at any rate, probably do.

SOCRATES: Very well. The people who desire bad things, according to you, but think that bad things harm whoever acquires them, presumably know that they will be harmed by them?

78a MENO: They must.

SOCRATES: But don't these people believe that those who are harmed are pitiful to the extent that they are harmed?

MENO: Again, they must.

SOCRATES: And that the pitiful are unhappy?

MENO: I think so.

SOCRATES: So is there anyone who wants to be pitiful and unhappy?

MENO: No, I don't believe so, Socrates.

SOCRATES: Therefore nobody wants bad things, Meno, assuming he doesn't want to be like that. For what else is being pitiful, if not desiring bad things and acquiring them?

MENO: It may be that what you're saying is true, Socrates, and that 78b
nobody wants bad things.

SOCRATES: Now weren't you just saying that virtue is both to want
good things and to be proficient?

MENO: Yes, I did.

SOCRATES: Isn't the part of your claim about 'wanting' true of everyone, so that in this respect at least one person is no better than another?

MENO: So it seems.

SOCRATES: Clearly, rather, if someone is better than another, he would
be better in respect of his proficiency.

MENO: Quite so.

SOCRATES: It seems then that what virtue is, according to your
account, is proficiency at securing good things for oneself. 78c

MENO: I believe, Socrates, that it is exactly as you now understand it.

SOCRATES: Then let's now see whether this claim of yours is true. For
you could perhaps be right. You say that virtue is being able to secure
good things?

MENO: Yes.

SOCRATES: And isn't it things such as health and wealth that you
describe as good?

MENO: Yes, and acquiring gold and silver, and political honours and
offices.

SOCRATES: By 'good things' you don't mean any things other than
those of this sort?

MENO: No, just everything of this sort. 78d

SOCRATES: Very well. So securing gold and silver is virtue, according
to Meno, family guest-friend of the Great King.[14] Do you add 'justly and
piously' to this securing, Meno? Or does it make no difference to you,
and even if someone secures them unjustly do you call it[*15] virtue all the
same?

MENO: No, surely not, Socrates.

SOCRATES: Rather you call it vice.

MENO: Quite so.

SOCRATES: Then it is necessary, it seems, to supplement this securing
with justice or temperance or piety, or with some other part of virtue. 78e
Otherwise it will not be virtue, even if it provides good things.

---

[14] The King of Persia.   [*15] Reading αὐτό at 78d6.

II

MENO: Right, for how could it come to be virtue without these?

SOCRATES: But what about *not* providing gold and silver, whenever it isn't just, either for oneself or for another? Isn't it virtue too, this failure to provide?[16]

MENO: It seems so.

SOCRATES: Therefore providing such goods wouldn't be virtue any more than the failure to provide them is. Instead, it seems, whatever is 79a done with justice will be virtue, but whatever is done without all such things will be vice.

MENO: I think it must be as you say.

SOCRATES: Now didn't we say a short while ago that each of these – justice and temperance and everything of that kind – was a part of virtue?

MENO: Yes.

SOCRATES: In that case, Meno, are you making fun of me?

MENO: How, Socrates?

SOCRATES: Because just now I asked you not to fragment virtue or chop it up, and provided models for you to follow in your reply. Yet you 79b have disregarded that and are telling me that virtue is the ability to secure good things with justice. And you say that justice is a part of virtue?

MENO: I do.

SOCRATES: Then from the points you admit it follows that virtue is doing whatever one does with a part of virtue. For you say that justice is a part of virtue, and that so is each of the others too. So why am I saying this? Because although I asked for an account of virtue as a whole, far from saying what it is itself, you claim that every action is virtue, provided that 79c it is done with a part of virtue, as if you had said what virtue is as a whole and I could already be expected to understand it, even if you chop it up into parts. So in my opinion, my dear Meno, you need to answer the same question again from the beginning: what is virtue, if every action would be virtue when done with a part of virtue? For that is what it means when someone says that every action done with justice is virtue. Or do you not believe that the same question needs to be tackled again, but instead think that someone knows what a part of virtue is, when he doesn't know what virtue itself is?

MENO: No, I don't think that.

---

[16] The Greek noun (*aporia*) translated as 'failure to provide' is translated as 'puzzlement' in 80a4.

SOCRATES: Right, and if you remember, when I gave you an answer 79d
about shape just now, I think we started discarding this sort of answer,
the sort that tries to respond through things which are still being searched
for and on which agreement has not yet been reached.

MENO: And we were right to do so, Socrates.

SOCRATES: Then you also, my friend, must not imagine that, when the
search is still under way for what virtue is as a whole, you will elucidate
virtue to anyone by giving your answer through its parts, or elucidate
anything else by speaking in this same way. Instead you must realise that 79e
the same question will again be required: what is the virtue about which
you make your claim? Or do you think there is nothing in what I say?

MENO: No, I think what you're saying is correct.

SOCRATES: So answer again from the beginning. What do you say
virtue is, both you and your associate?

MENO: Socrates, before I even met you I used to hear that all you do 80a
is get puzzled yourself and make others puzzled. And now, it seems to
me, you are bewitching me, drugging me and simply overwhelming me
with enchantment, so that I have been filled with puzzlement. If a little
humour is in order, what you comprehensively remind me of, both in
appearance and in other respects, is that marine creature, the electric ray.
For it makes anyone who approaches and touches it grow numb, and I
think you have now done something like that to me: my soul and mouth 80b
truly are numb, and I have no answer to give you. And yet I have made
lots of statements about virtue on countless occasions to many people,
and extremely well too, or so I thought. But now I don't have anything
at all to say even about what it is. And I think you are well advised in not
going away on voyages or spending time abroad, because if you were to
behave like this as a foreigner in another city, you would soon be arrested
as a magician.

SOCRATES: You have no scruples, Meno, and you nearly fooled me.

MENO: What exactly do you mean, Socrates?

SOCRATES: I know why you made that comparison about me. 80c

MENO: Why then, do you think?

SOCRATES: So that I would make one about you in return. I know this
about all beautiful people, that they enjoy being the subject of comparisons: it's to their advantage, because comparisons of beauties are also
beautiful, I think. But I won't reciprocate with a comparison of you. As
for me, if the ray itself is numb and that is how it makes others grow

numb as well, then I resemble it. If not, I don't. For I'm not well supplied with answers when I make other people puzzled. On the contrary, I am myself more puzzled than anybody, and that is how I make other people

80d puzzled as well. Regarding the present topic of what virtue is, I don't know the answer, and as for you, perhaps you did know it before you came into contact with me, but now you seem as if you didn't know it. All the same, I am ready to consider it with you and to share a search into what on earth it is.

MENO: And how will you search for something, Socrates, if you don't know at all what it is? What sort of thing from among those you don't know will you make the target of your search? Or even if you were to hit upon it with complete success, how will you know that *this* is the thing you didn't know?

80e SOCRATES: I understand what you mean to say, Meno. Do you see what an eristic argument you're spinning, that a person turns out not to be able to search either for what he knows or for what he doesn't know? For he wouldn't be searching for what he knows, since he knows it, and someone like that, at least, has no need to search; nor would he be searching for what he doesn't know, since in that case he doesn't even know what to search for.

81a MENO: Don't*[17] you think this argument a good one, Socrates?

SOCRATES: No, I don't.

MENO: Can you say in what way?

SOCRATES: Yes. I have heard both men and women who are wise about divine matters . . .

MENO: Saying what?

SOCRATES: A true statement, I think, and a noble one.

MENO: What is it, and who are the people who say it?

SOCRATES: Those who say it are all the priests and priestesses who

81b have taken care to be able to give an account of their practices. Pindar also says it, as do many other poets, all those that are divine. And what they say is this – consider whether you think it is true. They say that a person's soul is immortal, and at one time it meets its end – the thing they call dying – and at another time it is born again, but it never perishes. They say that, because of this, one should live one's whole life in the most holy

*[17] Reading οὔκουν at 81a1.

way possible. For from whoever

> Persephone accepts the atonement for ancient grief,
> in the ninth year she sends their soul*[18]
> up again to the sun above,
> and from them arise august kings 81c
> and men swift in might and matchless in wisdom;
> henceforth people call them holy heroes.

So since the soul both is immortal and has been born many times, and has seen both what is here and what is in Hades, and in fact all things, there is nothing it has not learned. And so it is no matter for wonder that it is possible for the soul to recollect both about virtue and about other things, given that it knew them previously. For since all nature is akin 81d and the soul has learned everything, there is no reason why someone who has recollected only one thing – which is what people call 'learning' – should not discover everything else, as long as one is brave and does not give up on the search. For seeking and learning turn out to be wholly recollection. Hence we must not be persuaded by that eristic argument, as it would make us lazy and is pleasant news to feeble people, whereas the present argument encourages us to search energetically. Because I 81e have confidence that it is true, I wish to join you in searching for what virtue is.

MENO: Yes, Socrates. But what do you mean by this claim that we don't learn, and that what we call 'learning' is recollection? Can you teach me that this is the case?

SOCRATES: I just said, Meno, that you're unscrupulous, and now 82a you're asking if I can 'teach' you – when I say that there is no teaching, only recollection. You're trying to make me be seen contradicting myself at the outset.

MENO: No, indeed, Socrates, I didn't say it with that in mind, but out of habit. Still, if there is some way you can demonstrate to me that it is as you say, then please do so.

SOCRATES: Well, it isn't an easy matter, but all the same I'm willing to make the effort for your sake. Please call over one of your many attendants 82b here, whichever one you like, so that I can display it for you in him.

MENO: Of course. Come here.

*[18] Reading ψυχάν at 81b10.

SOCRATES: Is he Greek and does he speak Greek?

MENO: Certainly – he was born in my house.

SOCRATES: Then pay attention and see which of these he seems to you to be doing: recollecting or learning from me.

MENO: I will.

SOCRATES: Tell me, boy, do you recognize that a square area is like this [ABCD]?

SLAVE: Yes.

82c   SOCRATES: So a square area is one with all these lines equal, all four of them?

SLAVE: Certainly.

SOCRATES: And doesn't it also have these equal lines across the middle [EF, GH]?

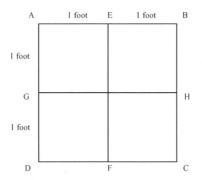

SLAVE: Yes.

SOCRATES: Now an area of this shape might come in different sizes?

SLAVE: Certainly.

SOCRATES: Well, suppose this side were two feet long and this side two feet, how many square feet would the whole area be? Consider it like this. If it were two feet in this direction, but only one foot in this direction, wouldn't the area be one times two square feet?

SLAVE: Yes.

82d   SOCRATES: But since it's two feet in this direction as well, doesn't it become two times two?

SLAVE: Yes, it does.

SOCRATES: So it becomes two times two square feet?

SLAVE: Yes.

SOCRATES: Then how many are two times two square feet? Work it out and tell me.

SLAVE: Four, Socrates.

SOCRATES: Now might there be another area double this one, but of the same shape, with all its lines equal, just like this one?

SLAVE: Yes.

SOCRATES: So how many square feet will it be?

SLAVE: Eight.

SOCRATES: Come on then, try to tell me how long each of its lines will be. For *this* one's lines were two feet. What about the line of that double area? 82e

SLAVE: Obviously double, Socrates.

SOCRATES: Do you see, Meno, how I'm teaching him nothing, but asking him everything? And now he thinks he knows the sort of line that will produce the area of eight square feet. Or don't you think so?

MENO: I do.

SOCRATES: Well, does he know?

MENO: Certainly not.

SOCRATES: And he thinks it will be produced by the double line?

MENO: Yes.

SOCRATES: Then watch him recollecting in order, just as one should recollect. But you, slave, answer me. Do you say that double the line produces double the area? I don't mean an area long in this direction but 83a short in that one – it must be equal in every direction, just like this area [ABCD], but double its size, eight square feet. Well, see whether you still believe that it will result from double the line.

SLAVE: Yes, I do.

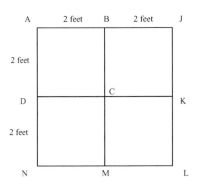

17

SOCRATES: Now does this line [AJ] become double the length of that one [AB] if we add another line of this length [BJ] from here [B]?

SLAVE: Certainly.

SOCRATES: So this line [AJ], you say, will produce the area of eight square feet, if there are four lines of this length?

83b SLAVE: Yes.

SOCRATES: Then let's draw four equal lines by extending it. Presumably this [AJLN] would be what you say is the area of eight square feet.

SLAVE: Of course.

SOCRATES: Now in it there are these four areas [ABCD, BJKC, CKLM, DCMN], each of which is equal to this area of four square feet [ABCD]?

SLAVE: Yes.

SOCRATES: So how large is it [AJLN]? Isn't it four times as large?

SLAVE: It must be.

SOCRATES: Well, is four times as large double?

SLAVE: Definitely not.

SOCRATES: But what multiple is it?

SLAVE: Quadruple.

83c SOCRATES: Therefore, boy, the double line produces not a double area but a quadruple one.

SLAVE: Yes, true.

SOCRATES: Because an area of four times four square feet has sixteen square feet. Right?

SLAVE: Yes.

SOCRATES: But what sort of line produces an area of eight square feet? Doesn't this line [AJ] produce a quadruple area?

SLAVE: I agree.

SOCRATES: And is this quarter*19 area here [ABCD] produced by this half line here [AB]?

SLAVE: Yes.

SOCRATES: Very well. And isn't the area of eight square feet double this area [ABCD], but half this one [AJLN]?

SLAVE: Yes.

SOCRATES: Won't it be produced by a line longer than one of that
83d length [AB], but shorter than one of this length [AJ]? No?

*19 Reading τέταρτον instead of τετράπουν at 83c5.

SLAVE: I believe so.

SOCRATES: Excellent – always reply by saying what you believe. Now tell me: wasn't this line [AB] two feet long, this one [AJ] four?

SLAVE: Yes.

SOCRATES: Therefore the line for the area of eight square feet must be greater than this two-foot line, but smaller than the four-foot.

SLAVE: It must.

SOCRATES: Try then to tell me how long you would say it is.   83e

SLAVE: Three feet.

SOCRATES: Now if it's to be three feet, shall we add on half of this line [AB] and make it three feet? For there are two feet here, one here. And from this point in the same way there are two feet here and one here. And so here we get the area you are speaking of.

SLAVE: Yes.

SOCRATES: Then if it were three feet in this direction and three in that one, does the whole area become three times three square feet?

SLAVE: So it seems.

SOCRATES: And three times three square feet is how many?

SLAVE: Nine.

SOCRATES: But the double area needed to be how many square feet?

SLAVE: Eight.

SOCRATES: So we still haven't got the area of eight square feet, not even from the line of three feet.

SLAVE: Certainly not.

SOCRATES: But what sort of line does produce it? Try to give us an accurate answer. And if you don't want to calculate its number, at any   84a
rate show us the right sort of line.

SLAVE: Honestly, Socrates, I don't know.

SOCRATES: Do you realise, Meno, what point he has by now reached in his recollection? At first he didn't know which is the line that bounds the area of eight square feet – just as he still doesn't know even now. But he nevertheless *thought* then that he knew it, and was answering confidently as if he knew, and didn't think he was puzzled. But by now he   84b
thinks that he is puzzled, and just as he doesn't know, so too he doesn't think he knows either.

MENO: Yes, true.

SOCRATES: Then is he now in a better state concerning the subject he didn't know?

MENO: Yes, that also seems the case to me.

SOCRATES: So when we made him puzzled and numb, as the ray does, we didn't do him any harm, did we?

MENO: I don't think so.

SOCRATES: In fact we've done him a service, it seems, in relation to the goal of discovering the truth about it. Now, that is, he really would be glad to search for it, as he doesn't know it, whereas then he would have thought that he could easily speak well both to many people and on many occasions about the double area, claiming that its side must be double in length.

84c

MENO: So it seems.

SOCRATES: So do you suppose that he would have attempted to search for or learn about what he believed he knew, though in fact he didn't know it, before the thought that he didn't know it made him plummet into puzzlement and crave the knowledge?

MENO: No, I don't think so, Socrates.

SOCRATES: Then the numbing benefited him?

MENO: I believe so.

SOCRATES: Watch then what he will actually discover as a result of this puzzlement, by searching with me, while I merely ask questions and don't teach him. But be on your guard to see whether you can catch me at any stage teaching him and expounding it to him, rather than asking for his opinions.

84d

Now, tell me. Isn't this our area of four square feet?[20] Do you understand?

SLAVE: I do.

SOCRATES: And could we add this second one, equal to it?

SLAVE: Yes.

SOCRATES: And this third one, equal to either of them?

SLAVE: Yes.

SOCRATES: Then might we add this one in the corner to complete our space?

SLAVE: Certainly.

SOCRATES: So presumably the result would be these four equal areas?

84e

SLAVE: Yes.

---

[20] Socrates now starts to draw four four-foot squares (ABCD, BJKC, CKLM and DCMN).

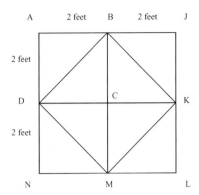

SOCRATES: Very well. What multiple is this total area [AJLN] of that one [ABCD]?

SLAVE: Quadruple.

SOCRATES: Yes, but we needed to get a double area. Or don't you remember?

SLAVE: Quite right.

SOCRATES: Now is there a line like this from corner to corner, cutting   85a
in two each of these areas?[21]

SLAVE: Yes.

SOCRATES: So we get these four equal lines, surrounding this area here [BKMD]?

SLAVE: Yes, we do.

SOCRATES: Examine it, then. What size is this area?

SLAVE: I don't follow.

SOCRATES: Each line has cut off the inside half of each of these four areas, hasn't it?

SLAVE: Yes.

SOCRATES: Then how many areas of this size [BCD] does it [BKMD] contain?

SLAVE: Four.

SOCRATES: But how many are there in this one [ABCD]?

SLAVE: Two.

SOCRATES: And four is what in relation to two?

SLAVE: Double.

SOCRATES: So how many square feet does this [BKMD] come out as?   85b

---

[21] Socrates now adds the diagonals forming the square BKMD.

SLAVE: Eight square feet.

SOCRATES: Produced by what sort of line?

SLAVE: By this one [BD].

SOCRATES: By the line extending from corner to corner in the area of four square feet?

SLAVE: Yes.

SOCRATES: Now the experts call this line a 'diagonal'. So if its name is 'diagonal', it is the diagonal according to you, Meno's slave, that would produce double the area.

SLAVE: Certainly, Socrates.

SOCRATES: What do you think, Meno? Is there any opinion he gave in reply which wasn't his own?

85c   MENO: No, they were his own.

SOCRATES: And yet he didn't know the answer, as we were saying a little earlier.

MENO: True.

SOCRATES: Right, but these opinions were inside him, weren't they?

MENO: Yes.

SOCRATES: Someone who doesn't have knowledge, then, whatever the things may be which he doesn't know, has in him true opinions about the very things he doesn't know?

MENO: It appears so.

SOCRATES: Yes, and now these opinions have only just been stirred up for him as if in a dream. But if someone goes on to question him about these things on many occasions and in many ways, you know that

85d   eventually he will have knowledge about them as precise as anyone's.

MENO: So it seems.

SOCRATES: So even though nobody has taught him but he has only been asked questions, will he possess knowledge, having himself retrieved the knowledge from himself?

MENO: Yes.

SOCRATES: And for him himself to retrieve knowledge in himself, isn't that recollecting?

MENO: Certainly.

SOCRATES: As for the knowledge which he now has, didn't he either acquire it at some time or have it always?

MENO: Yes.

SOCRATES: Now if he always had it, then he was always knowledgeable too. But if he acquired it at some time, he couldn't have done so in his present life, at any rate. Or has someone taught him to do geometry? For he will accomplish these same results in every branch of geometry, and in all the other disciplines.[22] So is there someone who has taught him everything? You're in a position to know, I suppose, especially since he was born and brought up in your house. 85e

MENO: I know that nobody ever taught him.

SOCRATES: Yet he has these opinions, doesn't he?

MENO: It seems he must have, Socrates.

SOCRATES: But if he didn't acquire them in his present life, isn't it immediately obvious that there was some other time at which he possessed them and had learned them? 86a

MENO: So it seems.

SOCRATES: Namely the time when he wasn't a human being?

MENO: Yes.

SOCRATES: So if there are going to be true opinions in him both for the time when he is a human being and for the time when he isn't, opinions which become knowledge when awoken by questioning, then for time everlasting won't his soul be in a state of having learned? Because obviously for the whole of time he either is or isn't a human being.

MENO: So it seems.

SOCRATES: Then if we always have in our soul the truth of things, wouldn't the soul be immortal, with the consequence that you should confidently try to search for and recollect what you don't know now – that is, what you don't remember? 86b

MENO: Somehow or other I think your point is a good one, Socrates.

SOCRATES: I think so too, Meno. In defence of the argument I would not affirm the other points very strongly, but that we would be better, more manly and less lazy by believing that one should search for what one doesn't know than if we believed that we cannot discover what we do not know and should not even search for it – that *is* something over which I would fiercely contend, if I were able, in both word and deed. 86c

MENO: Well, that also seems to me a good point, Socrates.

---

[22] The Greek word *mathēmata*, 'disciplines', is often used with special reference to the mathematical sciences.

SOCRATES: Now, given that we agree that one should search for what one doesn't know, do you want us to try to search together for what on earth virtue is?

MENO: Very much so. Actually, no, Socrates, what I would most enjoy considering and hearing about is what I asked at the start, whether

86d in trying this we should assume that virtue is teachable, or that people come to have it by nature, or that they acquire it in *what* way?

SOCRATES: If I controlled not only myself but you as well, Meno, we wouldn't have considered whether virtue is teachable or not teachable before we had first searched for what it is itself. But since you aren't even trying to control yourself – no doubt so that you may be 'free' – but are trying to control me, and actually *are* controlling me, I will give

86e in to you. What else can I do? So it seems we must consider what *sort* of thing something is, when we don't yet know *what* it is. If nothing else, at least release me a little from your control and agree to consider on a hypothesis whether it is teachable or whatever. By 'on a hypothesis' I mean the following. Take the way in which geometers often consider a question someone asks them, for example, whether it is possible for this

87a area to be inscribed as a triangle in this circle. One of them might say: 'I don't know yet whether the area is like that, but I think I have a sort of hypothesis, so to speak, which will be serviceable for our task. It is the following. If this area is such that, when someone has placed it alongside its given line, it falls short by the same sort of area as the very one that has been placed alongside, I think one result follows, and a different one if it is impossible for it to do this. So I want first to make this hypothesis,

87b and only then to tell you the result regarding its inscription in the circle, namely whether it is impossible or not.'[23] So too regarding virtue, since we don't know either what it is or what sort of thing it is, let us first make a hypothesis about it and then consider whether or not virtue is teachable, putting it like this: what sort of thing from among those connected with the soul must virtue be, if it is to be teachable or not teachable? First of all, if it is of a different kind from the sort of thing knowledge is, is it or isn't it teachable (or rather, as we were just saying, recollectable: let it

87c make no difference to us which of the two names we use). The question is: is it teachable? Or is this much obvious to everyone, that a person is taught nothing other than knowledge?

---

[23] See Dominic Scott, *Plato's Meno* (Cambridge, 2006), 135 for a suggested diagram.

MENO: I for one think so.

SOCRATES: And if virtue is a sort of knowledge, clearly it would be teachable.

MENO: Of course.

SOCRATES: Then we've quickly dealt with this point, that virtue is teachable if it's this kind of thing, but not if it's of the other kind.

MENO: Quite so.

SOCRATES: So next, it seems, we must consider whether virtue is knowledge or something different in kind from knowledge.

MENO: Yes, I think we should consider that next.   87d

SOCRATES: Well then, surely we say that virtue itself is good? And does this hypothesis hold for us, that it is good?

MENO: Certainly.

SOCRATES: Now if there is something else, distinct from knowledge, which also is good, then perhaps virtue might not be a sort of knowledge. But if there is nothing good that isn't included in knowledge, then we'd be right to suspect that virtue is a sort of knowledge.

MENO: True.

SOCRATES: And is it because of virtue that we are good?   87e

MENO: Yes.

SOCRATES: But if good, then beneficial. For all good things are beneficial, aren't they?

MENO: Yes.

SOCRATES: Then is virtue also something beneficial?

MENO: Necessarily, given what we have agreed.

SOCRATES: Let's consider, then, what sort of things benefit us, taking them one by one. Health, strength, beauty, and of course wealth: we say that these things and those like them are beneficial, don't we?

MENO: Yes.   88a

SOCRATES: Yet we speak of these same things as sometimes causing harm as well. Or do you speak otherwise?

MENO: No, I speak that way.

SOCRATES: Consider, then, what is that thing under whose guidance each of these things benefits us, and what is that thing under whose guidance each of them harms us? Isn't it under the guidance of right use that they benefit us, and without it that they harm us?

MENO: Certainly.

SOCRATES: Now next let's consider attributes of the soul as well. Are there things that you call temperance, justice, courage, speed of learning, memory, magnificence, and so on?

88b   MENO: There are.

SOCRATES: Consider this, then: out of these things, take those which you think aren't knowledge, but something other than knowledge – don't they sometimes harm, and sometimes benefit? Take courage, for example, if the courage in question isn't wisdom but some sort of boldness. Surely whenever a person is bold without understanding he is harmed, but when he is bold with understanding he is benefited?

MENO: Yes.

SOCRATES: Isn't it the same with both temperance and speed of learning? If learned and cultivated with understanding, they are beneficial, but if without understanding, harmful?

MENO: Very much so.

88c   SOCRATES: Then, in short, all the soul's acts of enterprise and endurance end in happiness when guided by wisdom, but in its opposite when guided by folly?

MENO: So it seems.

SOCRATES: Then if virtue is one of the things in the soul and if it is necessarily beneficial, then it must be wisdom, given that all the attributes of the soul are in themselves neither beneficial nor harmful, and that it is

88d   when wisdom or folly is added that they become harmful and beneficial. According to this argument, then, since virtue is beneficial it must be a sort of wisdom.

MENO: Yes, I think so.

SOCRATES: And besides, take those other things – wealth and the like – that we were just saying are sometimes good but sometimes harmful. Just as when wisdom guides the rest of the soul we said that it makes the things that belong to the soul beneficial, but that folly makes them harmful, so

88e   too in the case of these doesn't the soul make them beneficial when it uses and guides them correctly, but harmful when incorrectly?

MENO: Quite so.

SOCRATES: But it's the wise soul that guides correctly, and the foolish soul that guides mistakenly?

MENO: That's true.

SOCRATES: So we can make the following claim without exception: for a human being everything else depends on the soul, but the things that belong to the soul itself depend on wisdom, if they are going to be 89a good. And by this argument the beneficial would be wisdom. But do we say that virtue is beneficial?

MENO: Yes, certainly.

SOCRATES: Then do we say that virtue is wisdom, either the whole of wisdom or some part of it?

MENO: A good assertion, I think, Socrates.

SOCRATES: So if this is the case, good people wouldn't be good by nature.

MENO: No, I don't think so.

SOCRATES: Yes, for if they were the following would also happen, 89b I suppose. If the good became good by nature, presumably we would have people who recognized youngsters with good natures, and on their say-so we would take those youngsters in charge and guard them in the acropolis, sealing them up much more securely than our gold, to prevent anyone corrupting them, and to ensure that they became useful to cities when they came of age.

MENO: We probably would, Socrates.

SOCRATES: So since the good don't become good by nature, do they 89c do so by learning?

MENO: Yes, by now it's looking as if they must. And according to your hypothesis, Socrates, if virtue is knowledge, it is clear that virtue is teachable.

SOCRATES: Indeed it may be. But what if we were wrong to agree to that?

MENO: Well, it certainly seemed right just now.

SOCRATES: But I'm afraid that it must seem right not only 'just now', but also in the present and in the future, if there is to be anything sound about it.

MENO: Then just what is it? What do you have in mind that makes 89d you hesitate about it and suspect that virtue may not be knowledge?

SOCRATES: I'll tell you, Meno. Now I don't take back as incorrect the claim that it is teachable if it is knowledge. But whether it really *is* knowledge – just consider whether my misgivings about that seem reasonable to you. Tell me: if anything at all – not just virtue – is teachable, isn't it necessary that there be teachers and students of it?

MENO: Yes, I think so.

27

89e   SOCRATES: So, conversely, should something have neither teachers nor students, we'd be right to conjecture that it isn't teachable?

MENO: True. But don't you think there are teachers of virtue?

SOCRATES: Well, I've often searched to see whether there are any teachers of it, but in spite of all my efforts I can't discover them. Yet I've conducted the search together with many collaborators, and particularly with whichever people I think have most experience of the matter. And in fact right now, Meno, as luck would have it, Anytus[24] here has sat

90a   down with us. Let's invite him to take part in our search. It would only be reasonable for us to do so, since, first of all, Anytus here has a father, Anthemion, both rich and wise, who became rich not fortuitously or thanks to someone's gift (as happened to Ismenias of Thebes, who just recently acquired Polycrates' fortune) but because he won it with his own wisdom and diligence. Besides, he didn't seem conceited in his public life, or full of himself and offensive, but a decent and well-mannered

90b   man. Next, he brought up and educated Anytus well, to judge from the vote of the Athenian assembly – at any rate, they elect him to the highest offices. It's only right, then, to have collaborators like this in our search as to whether or not there are teachers of virtue, and who the teachers are. So, Anytus, do join in our search, together with both me and your guest Meno here, about who the teachers of this thing might be. Consider it

90c   in this way. If we wanted Meno here to become a good doctor, to whom would we send him for lessons? Wouldn't it be to the doctors?

ANYTUS: Yes, certainly.

SOCRATES: But what if we wanted him to become a good cobbler? Wouldn't we send him to the cobblers?

ANYTUS: Yes.

SOCRATES: And so on for the rest?

ANYTUS: Quite so.

SOCRATES: Then tell me again about the same cases but in the following way. In sending him to the doctors we say that we would be doing the right thing, if we wanted him to become a doctor. Now when we say

90d   this, do we mean that it would be sensible for us to send him to those who profess the craft rather than to those who don't, and to those who charge payment for this very thing, publicizing themselves as teachers of

---

[24] Anytus, a democratic politician, was to become three years later one of Socrates' two accusers in the trial which led to his execution. In what follows there are a number of veiled hints at his looming antagonism and its causes.

anyone who wants to come and learn? Aren't these the criteria we'd have to observe if we were going to school him correctly?

ANYTUS: Yes.

SOCRATES: Isn't the same true also of playing the reed-pipe and the like? If we want to make someone able to play the reed-pipe, it's extremely unintelligent to refuse to send him to those who undertake to teach the craft and who charge payment, but instead to bother other people,*25 who neither claim to be teachers nor have any student in the subject which we expect whoever we send to learn from them. Doesn't that seem very irrational to you? 90e

ANYTUS: Indeed it does, and ignorant to boot.

SOCRATES: Quite right. Well then, now you can join me in making plans about your guest, Meno here. You see, Anytus, he's long been telling me that he wants the wisdom and virtue that make people run both households and cities well, look after their own parents, and know both how to welcome citizens and foreign guests and how to send them on their way in a manner worthy of a good man. Concerning this virtue, then, consider to whom we'd be right to send him. Or is it in fact quite obvious, according to the argument we've just used, that it would be to those who claim to be teachers of virtue and publicize themselves as available to any Greek who wants to learn, charging an agreed price for the service? 91a 91b

ANYTUS: And just who do you mean by these, Socrates?

SOCRATES: You know as well as I do that they are those whom people call 'sophists'.

ANYTUS: Heavens, don't speak of them, Socrates! May no relative or friend of mine, from either this city or abroad, fall prey to such madness as to go to see those men and be ruined, because it's as plain as daylight that they are the ruin and corruption of those who associate with them. 91c

SOCRATES: What do you mean, Anytus? Out of all those who claim to know how to provide some beneficial service, are they alone so different from the rest that they not only don't improve whatever anyone entrusts to them, as the rest do, but actually, on the contrary, corrupt it? And in return for this do they openly assert the right to charge money? No, I don't see how I can believe you. For I know that one man, Protagoras,[26] 91d

---

*25 Deleting ζητοῦντα μανθάνειν παρὰ τούτων at 90e4.
[26] Protagoras of Abdera, a leading sophist, died c. 415 BC.

acquired more money from this wisdom than Pheidias,[27] who used to make artefacts of such conspicuous beauty, and ten other sculptors put together. And what you're saying is quite bizarre: those who work on

91e old shoes and mend clothes couldn't get away with it for a month if they returned the clothes and shoes in a worse condition than when they received them, but would soon starve to death if they behaved like this; and yet the whole of Greece didn't realize that for more than forty years Protagoras was corrupting those who associated with him and sending them on their way in a worse condition than when he took them in his charge (I think, you see, that he died when he was nearly seventy, and spent forty years in this profession) and in all that time and still to the present day he hasn't failed to be held in high regard. And that applies

92a not just to Protagoras, but to very many others as well, some who lived before him, others still alive even now. So according to you should we say that they knowingly deceive and ruin the young, or that they have taken themselves in as well? And will we reckon them to be as mad as that, when some say that they are the wisest of all people?

ANYTUS: They are far from being mad, Socrates. The mad ones are,

92b far rather, the young men who give them money, and, even more than these, those who entrust others to them[28] – their families, in other words. But maddest of all by far are the cities, for letting them enter and not expelling anyone, whether foreigner or citizen, who tries to behave in such a way.

SOCRATES: Has a sophist wronged you, Anytus? If not, why are you so angry with them?

ANYTUS: No, I assure you I've never yet even associated with any of them, and I wouldn't let anyone else connected with me do so either.

SOCRATES: Then you're completely without experience of these men?

ANYTUS: Yes, and I hope to stay that way.

92c SOCRATES: You astonish me – how could you know whether this creature contains any good or bad, if you were completely without experience of it?

ANYTUS: Easily. Whether or not I am without experience of them, I do at least know who they are.

---

[27] The most celebrated Athenian sculptor.
[28] The Greek could also be translated 'those who allow them', that is, those who allow the young to pay to see sophists.

SOCRATES: Perhaps you're a clairvoyant, Anytus. For, given what you yourself say, I'd wonder how else you know about them. But in any case, we're not trying to find out who the people are who would put Meno in a poor condition if he went to see them – let these be the sophists, if you want. Tell us rather about the other ones, and assist your family friend here by explaining to him who in this enormous city would, if he went to see them, make him outstanding in the virtue I was just describing.

ANYTUS: Why don't *you* explain it to him?

SOCRATES: Well, I have said who I thought were teachers of these things, but it turns out that there isn't anything in what I'm saying, according to you. And perhaps there is something in what you're saying. But then you, in your turn, please tell him to which Athenians he should go. Tell him the name of whoever you want.

ANYTUS: Why need he be told the name of an individual? Whichever Athenian of noble character he meets, none will fail to make him better than the sophists would, provided that he's willing to do as they say.

SOCRATES: Did these men of noble character become like this fortuitously, and although they haven't learned from anyone, can they none the less teach others what they themselves haven't learned?

ANYTUS: These too, I reckon, learned from the previous generation, who were themselves of good character. Or don't you think there have been many good men in this city?

SOCRATES: I think, Anytus, that there are men here who are good at running the city, and, what's more, that there have been such men in the past just as much as there are now. But have they really been good *teachers* of their own virtue as well? This, you see, is what our discussion is about. Not whether there are good men here or not, nor if there have been before, but whether virtue is teachable – that is what we have long been considering. And in doing so we're considering the following: whether the good men, both of this generation and of the previous one, also knew how to pass on to someone else this virtue in which they themselves were good, or whether it is something that cannot be passed on by a human being[29] nor received by one from another. That is what Meno and I have long been seeking. So on the basis of what you yourself say, consider it as follows. Wouldn't you say that Themistocles[30] was a good man?

92d

92e

93a

93b

93c

---

[29] The mention of 'human beings' may anticipate the suggestion of *divine* allocation in 99c–100b.
[30] Athenian statesman, *c.* 524–459 BC.

ANYTUS: I certainly would, he most of all.

SOCRATES: And would you say that he was a good teacher as well –
that if anyone else was a teacher of his own virtue, then Themistocles
certainly was one?

ANYTUS: Yes, I think so, if he actually wanted to be.

SOCRATES: But do you suppose that he wouldn't have wanted others
to become of noble character, especially his own son? Or do you think he
93d   was grudging towards his son and deliberately didn't pass on the virtue in
which he himself was good? Haven't you heard that Themistocles had his
son, Cleophantus, taught to be a good horseman? At any rate, Cleophantus
used to stand upright on horseback and keep his balance, and throw the
javelin from horseback when standing upright, and perform many other
amazing things. Themistocles had had him taught those things, and
made him wise in everything that depended on good teachers. Haven't
you heard that from your seniors?

ANYTUS: I have.

SOCRATES: Then nobody would have criticized his son's nature as no
good.

93e   ANYTUS: Probably not.

SOCRATES: But what about this? To this day have you ever heard from
anyone, younger or older, that Cleophantus, the son of Themistocles, was
a good and wise man in the things in which his father was?

ANYTUS: Certainly not.

SOCRATES: So do we suppose that while he wanted to educate his own
son in those other things, he didn't want to make him any better than his
neighbours in the sort of wisdom in which he himself was wise – if virtue
really is, as we were saying,[31] teachable?

ANYTUS: Quite probably he didn't.

SOCRATES: Then you can see the sort of teacher of virtue *he* made, and
you yourself agree that he was the best of those of previous generations.
94a   But now let's consider someone else – Aristides,[32] the son of Lysimachus.
Don't you agree that he was good?

ANYTUS: Yes, absolutely.

SOCRATES: Didn't he too educate his own son, Lysimachus, best of
all the Athenians in everything that depended on teachers? But do you
think he has made him a better man than anyone else? For you've actually

---

[31] At 89c.   [32] Athenian statesman, died *c.* 467 BC; known as 'Aristides the Just'.

associated with him, I believe, and can observe what sort of man he is. Or, if you like, take Pericles,[33] a man of such magnificent wisdom – do   94b you know that he brought up two sons, Paralus and Xanthippus?

ANYTUS: I do.

SOCRATES: Well you know as well as I do that he taught them to equal any Athenian as horsemen, and educated them to equal anyone in music, athletics, and everything else that depends on expertise. But in spite of that did he have no wish to make them good men? He did, I think, but I suspect that that isn't teachable. And to stop you thinking that only a few Athenians and the worst of them were unable to do this, note that   94c Thucydides[34] also brought up two sons, Melesias and Stephanus, and educated them well in everything, and in particular made them the finest wrestlers in Athens, because he sent one to Xanthias and the other to Eudorus. They were thought to be the finest wrestlers of their day – don't you remember?

ANYTUS: I do, from hearsay.

SOCRATES: Then isn't it obvious that he would never have taught his sons that for which he had to pay for their teaching, yet failed to teach   94d them that on which he didn't have to spend anything, namely making them good men, if it were teachable? But maybe Thucydides was a bad sort, and didn't have a huge number of friends among the Athenians and the allies? Well, he came from a great family and had great influence in this city and among the other Greeks, so that if this were teachable, he would have discovered someone, local or foreign, who could be expected to make his sons good, supposing he himself lacked the time because of   94e his public commitments. But anyhow, Anytus, my friend, I suspect that virtue isn't teachable.

ANYTUS: Socrates, you seem to me to find it an easy matter to speak ill of people. So I'd advise you to be cautious, if you're willing to take my advice. There may be other cities too where it is easier to do ill to people than good, but in this city it certainly is. And I believe you yourself know   95a that as well.

SOCRATES: Meno, I think Anytus is angry, and I'm not at all surprised. For first he thinks that I'm casting a slur on these men, and second he considers himself to be one of them. If he ever realises what it's really

---

33 Leading Athenian statesman, *c.* 495–429 BC.
34 Not the historian of that name, but Thucydides son of Melesias, *c.* 508–425 BC, Athenian states-man.

like to 'speak ill', he'll stop being angry, but at the moment he doesn't know. As for you, tell me, aren't there men of noble character among your people as well?

MENO: Certainly.

95b SOCRATES: Well then, are they willing to present themselves as teachers for the young, and to agree that they are teachers, or*35 that virtue is teachable?

MENO: Indeed not, Socrates – sometimes you'd hear from them that it's teachable, sometimes than it's not.

SOCRATES: So should we say that they are teachers of this subject, if they don't agree even about this?

MENO: No, I don't think so, Socrates.

SOCRATES: Very well. Do you think that those sophists, the only people who profess it, are teachers of virtue?

95c MENO: That's just what I admire most about Gorgias, Socrates, that you'd never hear him promising this. He even laughs at the other sophists when he hears them promising it. Instead it's at speaking that he thinks he should make people clever.

SOCRATES: So you don't think that the sophists are teachers either?

MENO: I can't say, Socrates. You see, I myself have the same experience as most people: sometimes I think so, sometimes I don't.

SOCRATES: But are you aware that it's not only you and other members of the public who sometimes think that it's teachable, sometimes that it's

95d not, but do you know that the poet Theognis[36] also says the very same?

MENO: In which verses?

SOCRATES: In his elegiacs, where he says:

> Drink and eat beside them, sit among them,
> Amuse them – if their power is great.
> From good men you will be taught good things. But if you keep
95e > Bad company, you will lose even what sense you have.

Do you notice that in these verses he talks as if virtue were teachable?

MENO: He does seem to.

SOCRATES: But in other verses his position changes slightly:

---

*35 Reading ἤ instead of the second καί at 95b2.

[36] Sixth-century BC elegiac poet from Megara. At 95d–e Socrates quotes lines 33–6 in the modern collection of Theognis' surviving poetry; in 95e–96a, lines 434–8.

If understanding (he says) could be created and inserted into a
man,

He claims, I think, that those who could do this

Would earn many large rewards,

And that

No bad son would ever issue from a good father,
If he obeys sound-minded advice. But with teaching   96a
You will never make the bad man good.

Do you realize that he contradicts himself on the same subject?

MENO: So it seems.

SOCRATES: Can you then name any other subject whose professed
teachers are not only not agreed to be teachers of other people, but aren't
even agreed to know it themselves, but are thought to be worthless in the   96b
very subject whose teachers they claim to be, while those who are agreed
to be of noble character themselves sometimes say that it is teachable,
sometimes that it isn't? When people are so confused about something,
would you say that they are genuinely its teachers?

MENO: No, indeed.

SOCRATES: Then if neither the sophists nor those who are themselves
of noble character are teachers of the subject, isn't it clear that others
wouldn't be?

MENO: I don't think they would.

SOCRATES: Right, and if there are no teachers, there are no students   96c
either?

MENO: I think it is as you say.

SOCRATES: And we've agreed that if a subject has neither teachers nor
students, then it isn't[*37] teachable?

MENO: We have.

SOCRATES: Now there appear to be no teachers of virtue anywhere?

MENO: That's true.

SOCRATES: Right, and if there are no teachers, there are no students
either?

MENO: It appears that way.

SOCRATES: Then virtue can't be teachable?

[*37] Reading μή instead of μηδέ in 96c4.

96d MENO: It seems not, if our investigation has been correct. As a result, Socrates, I actually wonder whether good men may even be non-existent, or what the process could be by which people come to be good.

SOCRATES: In all likelihood, Meno, you and I are inferior sorts, Gorgias having educated you inadequately, and Prodicus[38] me. Above all, then, let's turn our attention to ourselves and seek someone who will

96e make us better in some way or other. I say this with our recent search in mind, thinking how we ridiculously failed to notice that it is not only when knowledge guides them that people run their affairs correctly and well. Doubtless it is in this way that knowledge is eluding us of how good men ever come to be.

MENO: What do you mean by this, Socrates?

SOCRATES: The following. 'Good men must be beneficial' – that is

97a something about which we are correct to have agreed that it could not be otherwise. Or isn't it?

MENO: Yes, it is.

SOCRATES: And also 'they will be beneficial, if they guide us correctly in our affairs' – to this too, I take it, we were right to agree?

MENO: Yes.

SOCRATES: But 'it is impossible to guide correctly unless one is wise' – on that it looks as if we haven't agreed correctly.

MENO: Just what do you mean?

SOCRATES: I'll tell you. If someone knew the way to Larisa or to wherever else you like, and walked there and guided others, wouldn't he guide them correctly and well?

MENO: Certainly.

97b SOCRATES: But what if someone had the correct opinion about which way it is, but hadn't gone there and didn't have knowledge about it – wouldn't he also guide people correctly?

MENO: Certainly.

SOCRATES: And, I suppose, as long as he has correct opinion about the things of which the other has knowledge, he'll have true beliefs, albeit without wisdom, and be no worse a guide than the one who is wise on the matter.

---

[38] Cf. n. 12 above. In the *Cratylus* (384b) Socrates says that he attended Prodicus' class on the 'correctness of names', but only the cut-price version.

MENO: Yes, no worse.

SOCRATES: True opinion is therefore no worse a guide than wisdom for correctness of action. And it is this that we were overlooking just now in our consideration of what sort of thing virtue is, when we said that wisdom alone guides correct action. It turns out that there was true   97c
opinion as well.

MENO: It does seem that way.

SOCRATES: Then correct opinion isn't any less beneficial than knowledge.

MENO: Well, there's at least this much difference, Socrates – someone with knowledge would succeed all the time, whereas someone with correct opinion would sometimes succeed, sometimes not.

SOCRATES: What do you mean? If someone had correct opinion all the time, wouldn't he succeed all the time, for as long as his opinions were correct?

MENO: That does seem necessary to me. It makes me wonder, Socrates, why on earth, if so, knowledge is much more precious than correct   97d
opinion, and what makes the two of them different.

SOCRATES: Do you know the reason why you wonder this, or shall I tell you?

MENO: Do by all means tell me.

SOCRATES: It is because you haven't paid attention to the statues of Daedalus.[39] Perhaps they don't even exist in your part of the world.

MENO: What is your point?

SOCRATES: That they too run away and escape if they haven't been tied down, but stay with one if they have been.

MENO: And what of that?   97e

SOCRATES: Owning one of his products isn't of much value if it's untied, like a runaway, because it doesn't stay with one. But it is worth a lot if it is tied down. For his works are very beautiful. So what is my point? It's about true opinions. For true opinions are also a thing of beauty, as long as they stay with one, and all their consequences are   98a
good. But they're not prepared to stay with one for long. Instead they run away from the person's soul. As a result, they are not worth very much until someone ties them down by reasoning out the cause. And

---

[39] Legendary craftsman and inventor, whom Socrates elsewhere claims as an ancestor.

this, Meno, my friend, is recollection, as we have earlier agreed. When they've been tied down, they become, first of all, instances of knowledge, and, secondly, settled. It's precisely for this reason that knowledge is something more precious than correct opinion, and it's being tied down that makes knowledge different from correct opinion.

MENO: Yes, Socrates, it does indeed look that way.

98b SOCRATES: And yet I myself don't say this in the belief that I know it, but rather as a conjecture. But as for the claim that correct opinion and knowledge are different in kind, about that I certainly don't think I'm making a conjecture, but if I'd claim to know anything – and there are few things of which I would claim this – I'd at all events include this among the things I know.

MENO: Yes, and you're correct to say this.

SOCRATES: Very well. Isn't it also correct to say that when true opinion is our guide it makes the result of each action no worse than knowledge does?

MENO: Here too what you say seems true to me.

98c SOCRATES: So correct opinion will be in no way worse than knowledge and no less beneficial for actions, nor will the man with correct opinions be any worse or less beneficial than the one with knowledge.

MENO: That's true.

SOCRATES: And it's the good man whom we've agreed to be beneficial.

MENO: Yes.

SOCRATES: Then since it's not only because of knowledge that men would be good and beneficial to their cities, if they were, but also because

98d of correct opinion, and since people have neither knowledge nor true opinion*40 by nature . . . Or does it seem to you that they have either of them by nature?

MENO: No, it doesn't.

SOCRATES: Since, then, people don't have them by nature, the good couldn't be good by nature either.

MENO: Certainly not.

SOCRATES: Right, and it is because they aren't so by nature that we were considering the next option, namely whether it's teachable.

MENO: Yes.

*40 Deleting οὔτ᾽ ἐπίκτητα at 98d1.

SOCRATES: Didn't we think that if virtue is wisdom it is teachable?

MENO: Yes.

SOCRATES: Yes, and that if it were teachable, it would be wisdom?

MENO: Certainly.

SOCRATES: Right, and that if there were teachers of it, it would be 98e
teachable, but if not, it wouldn't be teachable?

MENO: Quite so.

SOCRATES: But we've agreed that there are no teachers of it?

MENO: That's right.

SOCRATES: So we've agreed that it is neither teachable nor wisdom?

MENO: Yes, absolutely.

SOCRATES: And yet we agree that it's good, at any rate?

MENO: Yes.

SOCRATES: And that that which guides correctly is beneficial and
good?

MENO: Yes, certainly.

SOCRATES: Right, and that there are only these two things which guide 99a
correctly, true opinion and knowledge, and that with them a human being
guides correctly. What happens correctly because of some kind of luck
doesn't do so by human guidance. But in cases where humankind guides
matters to the correct outcome, it is these two things, true opinion and
knowledge, that do it.

MENO: I think so.

SOCRATES: So since it isn't teachable, it no longer looks as if virtue is
knowledge?

MENO: No, it doesn't seem to.

SOCRATES: And so out of the two things that are good and beneficial 99b
one has been eliminated, and knowledge can't be our guide in political
action.

MENO: I don't think so.

SOCRATES: And therefore it was not by some sort of wisdom nor
because they were wise that men such as Themistocles and his circle, and
those Anytus here just mentioned, guided their cities. And it is for this
very reason that they are unable to make others the sort of men that they
themselves are, in that it is not because of knowledge that they are like
this.

MENO: It seems to be as you say, Socrates.

99c SOCRATES: So if this doesn't happen by knowledge, the remaining alternative is that it happens by good opinion. Politicians use this when they make their cities run correctly, and, as far as wisdom goes, they're no different from oracles and prophets. For these latter also say many true things when inspired, but they know none of the things they say.

MENO: Probably so.

SOCRATES: So, Meno, should we call 'divine' these men who, without understanding, act and speak correctly in many important matters?

MENO: Definitely.

99d SOCRATES: Then we'd be correct to call 'divine' the oracles and prophets we just mentioned, and all the poetic types as well. And we'd say that the politicians are not the least divine and inspired of these, inspirited and possessed as they are by god, when they speak correctly in many important matters, despite knowing nothing of what they're saying.

MENO: Certainly.

SOCRATES: Yes, Meno, and of course women call good men 'divine'. And whenever the Spartans extol someone as a good man, they say 'A divine man, that one'.

99e MENO: Right, Socrates, and they do seem to be correct in what they say. But perhaps Anytus here is annoyed by what you're saying.

SOCRATES: I'm not at all concerned about that. We'll have a conversation with him on a later occasion, Meno. But if on the present occasion we have both searched and spoken well throughout our discussion, the result would be that virtue neither comes by nature nor is teachable, but that whoever acquires it would do so by divine allocation without under-

100a standing, unless there were a politician capable of making another man a politician as well. If there were, he could more or less be described as the same sort of person among the living as Homer said Teiresias is among the dead, when he said: 'He alone' (of all those in Hades) 'retains his understanding, but the others scurry about as shades.'[41] Likewise here as well a man like that would be, so to speak, the real thing compared with shades as regards virtue.

100b MENO: I think you make an excellent point, Socrates.

SOCRATES: Then on the basis of this reasoning, Meno, it seems to us that whoever acquires virtue does so by divine allocation. But the time when we'll know the plain truth about it will be when, before considering

---

[41] *Odyssey* 10.495. Teiresias, a Theban, was a mythical blind seer.

in what way people acquire virtue, we first attempt to search for what on earth virtue is, in and of itself. But now the time has come for me to go somewhere. As for you, please persuade your host Anytus here of the same things of which you yourself have been persuaded, so that he may be a gentler person. For if you persuade him, you'll be doing the   100c Athenians a service as well.

Phaedo

57a   ECHECRATES:[1] Were you with Socrates yourself, Phaedo, on the day he drank the poison in prison, or did you hear about it from someone else?

PHAEDO:[2] I was there myself, Echecrates.

ECHECRATES: So what did he say before his death? And how did he meet his end? I'd enjoy hearing about it, you see. For, as a matter of fact, scarcely any citizens of Phlius visit Athens these days, and no foreigner
57b   who could give us a clear report about it has come from there for a long time. Other than that he died from drinking poison, that is. They couldn't tell us anything else.

58a   PHAEDO: So haven't you even found out how the trial went?

ECHECRATES: Yes, someone did give us a report about that, and we really were surprised that evidently he died long after it had finished. So why was that, Phaedo?

PHAEDO: It was a matter of chance, Echecrates, in his case. For by chance on the day before his trial the stern of the ship the Athenians send to Delos had been wreathed.

ECHECRATES: What ship is that?

PHAEDO: It's the ship in which, according to the Athenians, Theseus
58b   once set out to Crete with the famous 'twice seven', and both saved their lives and escaped with his own. Anyway, as the story goes, at that time they had vowed to Apollo that if they were saved, in return they would send an embassy to Delos every year. And this is the embassy they have

---

[1] Echecrates of Phlius, a member of the Pythagorean community at Phlius in the early to mid-fourth century.
[2] Phaedo of Elis, a Socratic philosopher of some note who wrote dialogues and founded his own school.

always sent the god each year from that time, and still do now. Well, once they have started the embassy they have a law that during that time the city should be kept pure, and so the people should put nobody to death, until the ship has reached Delos and come back to Athens again. But this sometimes takes a long time, if winds chance to hold them up. The 58c embassy starts the moment the priest of Apollo wreaths the stern of the ship; and as chance would have it this had happened, as I said, on the day before the trial. It was for these reasons that Socrates had a long time in prison between his trial and his death.

ECHECRATES: What then about the details of his actual death, Phaedo? What was it that was said and done, and which of his friends were with him? Or would the officials not let them see him, so that he met his end without the company of loved ones?

PHAEDO: Not at all. Some of them were with him – many, in fact. 58d

ECHECRATES: Then do your best to give us the clearest report you can of all this, unless you happen to be busy.

PHAEDO: No, I'm not busy, and I'll try to describe it to you all. For remembering Socrates, both when I'm doing the talking and when I hear about him from someone else, is always the greatest pleasure of all for me.

ECHECRATES: The same goes for your audience, Phaedo. Try to go through every detail as accurately as you can.

PHAEDO: Of course. My own experiences when I was with him were 58e surprising. For pity didn't enter me, as you might have expected, given that I was witnessing the death of a friend. The man seemed to me to be happy, Echecrates, both in his behaviour and in what he said, so fearlessly and nobly did he meet his end. So the thought came to me that even his going to Hades was not without divine benefaction, and also that when he arrived there he would fare well, if anyone ever did. For these reasons 59a hardly any feeling of pity entered me, as you would expect of someone at a scene of misfortune; nor did I feel any pleasure that we were caught up in philosophy, as our custom had been – for in fact our conversation was a philosophical one. Instead I had a quite peculiar experience, an unusual mixture blended together from both the pleasure and the pain, as I took in the fact that his life was just about to end. Everyone present was pretty much in this state, sometimes laughing, but at other times in tears, and one of us particularly so, Apollodorus – I suppose you know the man and 59b the way he behaves.

ECHECRATES: Yes, of course.

PHAEDO: Well, he was completely like that, and I myself was in turmoil, as the others were too.

ECHECRATES: Who in fact was there, Phaedo?

PHAEDO: Of the locals there was the Apollodorus I've mentioned, of course, and Critobulus and his father,[3] and then Hermogenes, Epigenes, Aeschines and Antisthenes. Ctesippus of the Paeanian deme was there as well, and Menexenus and some other locals. But Plato[4] was ill, I think.

ECHECRATES: Were any foreigners there?

59c PHAEDO: Yes: Simmias of Thebes, along with Cebes[5] and Phaedondes, and from Megara Euclides[6] and Terpsion.

ECHECRATES: What about Aristippus and Cleombrotus? Were they there?

PHAEDO: No, they weren't. They were said to be in Aegina.

ECHECRATES: And was anyone else there?

PHAEDO: I think these were pretty much all of them.

ECHECRATES: Well then, what discussions were there, can you tell me?

PHAEDO: I'll try to describe everything to you from the beginning.
59d You see, we'd been in the habit of visiting Socrates on a regular basis, particularly on the preceding days, both I and the others. We used to assemble from dawn at the court where the trial itself had been held, because it was near the prison. So each day we would wait around until the prison opened, passing the time with one another, as it didn't open early. But when it did open, we'd go in to see Socrates and usually spent the day with him. And on that occasion we'd assembled at an earlier
59e time, because as we left the prison the evening before, we found out that the ship had arrived from Delos. So we sent round a message to get to the usual place as early as possible. We arrived, and the door-keeper who usually let us in came out and told us to wait and not enter until

---

3 Crito, Socrates' faithful old friend, and sole interlocutor in Plato's *Crito*.
4 One of only three self-mentions by Plato in his dialogues. The other two are at *Apology* 34a and 38b, where he is named as being present at Socrates' trial.
5 Simmias and Cebes, who turn out to be the principal interlocutors of the dialogue, were Thebans who had studied with the Pythagorean Philolaus as well as being members of Socrates' circle. Cebes, at least, lived until the mid-fourth century, and both are reported to have written philosophical dialogues.
6 Euclides of Megara, Socratic philosopher and founder of the Megaric school of philosophy, which in turn exercised a strong influence on Stoicism. After Socrates' execution, Plato and other Socratics were said to have taken refuge with him at Megara.

he himself gave the word: 'The Eleven,'[7] he explained, 'are unchaining
Socrates and giving orders for him to die today.' But it wasn't long before
he came back and told us to go in. So in we went and, as we did so, we
found Socrates newly unchained, and Xanthippe[8] – you know her, of
course – holding his child and sitting by his side. When Xanthippe saw
us, she cried out and said just the sort of thing that women tend to say:
'Socrates, this is now the very last time that your friends will speak to
you and you to them.' Socrates turned to Crito and said: 'Crito, someone
had better take her home.'

Some of Crito's people started to take her away, crying and beating
herself in her grief. But Socrates, sitting up onto his couch, bent his
leg and gave it a hard rub with his hand, and as he rubbed it he said:
'What a peculiar thing it seems to be, my friends, this thing that people
call "pleasure". What a surprising natural relation it has to its apparent
opposite, pain. I mean that the two of them refuse to come to a person
at the same time, yet if someone chases one and catches it he is pretty
much forced always to catch the other one too, as if they were two things
but joined by a single head. And I do believe,' he said, 'that if Aesop
had reflected on them, he would have composed a fable: that they were
at war, and that god wanted to reconcile them, and that, finding himself
unable to do so, he joined their heads together, the result being that if
one of them comes to somebody the other too will later follow in its
train. That is precisely what seems to be happening to me too. Because
pain was in my leg from the fetter, pleasure seems to have come in its
train.'

Cebes took this up: 'Indeed, Socrates,' he said, 'thanks for reminding
me. You know those poems you've been composing, your versifications
of Aesop's tales and the proem to Apollo? Well, some people were already
asking me about them, and in particular Evenus[9] asked the day before
yesterday what on earth your idea was in composing them when you came
here, given that you had never composed poetry before. So if you care
at all about my having an answer for Evenus when he asks me again –
because I'm quite sure that he will ask – tell me what to say.'

'Well,' he said, 'tell him the truth, Cebes: that when I composed them it
wasn't because I wanted to rival his expertise or that of his poems, which

60a

60b

60c

60d

60e

[7] The panel of officers, chosen by lot, who enforced the sentences decided in Athenian courts.
[8] Socrates' wife.
[9] Evenus of Paros, poet and rhetorician.

I knew was no easy task. No, there were some dreams whose meaning I was testing, and thus honouring a sacred obligation, just in case it might after all be this sort of music that they were ordering me to compose. Here is what they were like. The same dream has often visited me in my past life, appearing in different guises at different times, but saying the same things. "Socrates," it said, "compose music and work at it." In the past I used to suppose that it was encouraging me and cheering

61a me on to do what I *was* doing, like those who cheer runners. I took the dream to be cheering me on in the same way to do just what I was doing, composing music, on the grounds that philosophy is the greatest music, and that that was what I was doing. But now since the trial was over and the god's festival was holding up my death, I thought that just in case the dream might after all be instructing me to compose music as commonly understood, I should not disobey it but should start

61b composing. For it seemed safer not to depart before I had honoured my sacred obligation by composing poems in obedience to the dream. So that is how I came to start by making a composition dedicated to the god whose festival was currently being held. But, after I had attended to the god, I reflected that the poet, if he is to be a poet, should compose stories, not arguments. I myself was not a story-teller, so I took the stories I had ready to hand and knew, those of Aesop, and made compositions out of the ones that first came to mind. So, Cebes, tell all this to Evenus, give him my best wishes and tell him, if he is in his right mind, to come

61c after me as soon as possible. I leave, it seems, today: so the Athenians command.'

To which Simmias said: 'Fancy recommending a thing like that to Evenus, Socrates! I've often encountered him in the past, and from what I've seen I imagine there's no way that he will follow your advice willingly.'

'Really?' said he. 'Isn't Evenus a philosopher?'

'I think he is,' said Simmias.

'Then Evenus will be willing, as will everyone who has a worthy claim to this activity. Though perhaps he won't use violence on himself, for

61d they say that it isn't sanctioned.' As he was saying this he put his legs down on the ground, and spent the rest of the conversation sitting in that position.

Cebes then put a question to him. 'What do you mean by this, Socrates – that it isn't sanctioned to use violence on oneself, but that the philosopher would be willing to follow someone who is dying?'

'What, Cebes? Haven't you and Simmias heard about such things from your dealings with Philolaus?'[10]

'Nothing clear, at any rate, Socrates.'

'Well, I too speak about them from hearsay. I'll gladly tell you what I happen to have heard. Besides, it may be particularly appropriate for someone about to travel there to consider thoroughly and tell stories about what we think the stay there is like. For what else is there to do to fill the time until sunset?' 61e

'Then why ever do they say that it isn't sanctioned to kill oneself, Socrates? For actually – going back to what you just asked – I did hear from Philolaus, while he was living with us, and in fact from some other people too, that one shouldn't do this. But as yet nobody has ever told me anything clear about these issues.'

'Still, you mustn't despair,' he said, 'because you may actually get to hear something clear. However, maybe it will seem surprising to you if this and nothing else is simple – if, that is, it never happens for humankind that, as in other matters, at certain times and for certain people it is better to be dead than alive; and as for those for whom it is better to be dead, maybe it seems surprising to you if it is impious for these people to benefit themselves, but they must wait for someone else to be their benefactor.' 62a

Cebes chuckled at that. 'Zeus be my witness,' he said, speaking in his own dialect.

'Yes, and it would seem unreasonable,' said Socrates, 'at least when put like that. But still perhaps there really is something to be said for it. Now what is said in secret accounts about these matters, that we human beings are in a sort of prison[11] and that one must not release oneself from it or run away, that seems to me a weighty saying and one that is not easy to penetrate. But all the same, Cebes, this at least does strike me as well said, that it is gods who take care of us and that we human beings are one of the gods' possessions. Or do you not think so?' 62b

'I do,' said Cebes.

'Well,' said he, 'supposing one of *your* possessions were to kill itself but you hadn't given a sign that you wanted it to die, wouldn't*[12] you be 62c

<hr>

[10] Philolaus of Croton (*c.* 470–*c.* 385 BC) was the major Pythagorean philosopher of the late fifth century. See further, n. 41 below.

[11] The Greek word translated 'prison' also means 'garrison'.

*[12] Reading οὔκουν at 62c1.

angry with it, and if you had some way of punishing it, wouldn't you do so?'

'Certainly,' he said.

'So perhaps in this way it isn't unreasonable that one should not kill oneself until god imposes some necessity, like the necessity now facing us.'

'Yes,' said Cebes, 'this, at least, seems plausible. On the other hand, what you were saying just now, that philosophers would be ready and
62d willing to die, that looks odd, Socrates, if in fact what we were saying just now is reasonable: both that it is god who takes care of us and that we are his possessions. For it is unreasonable that the wisest people shouldn't resent leaving this ministration, in which they are supervised by the best supervisors there are, namely gods. Because, I take it, such a person doesn't think that *he* will take better care of himself after he has become
62e free. An unintelligent person, however, might well think so, namely that he should try to escape from his master. He wouldn't reflect that he should not do so, from a good one at least, but rather should do his best to stay with him. Because of that he would try to escape without pausing to reflect. But someone with intelligence would surely desire always to be with his better. And yet put like this, Socrates, it's likely that the truth is the opposite of what was just said: it's fitting that the wise should resent dying, the foolish welcome it.'

63a When Socrates heard this he seemed to me delighted by Cebes' persistence, and he looked at us and said: 'As you can see, Cebes is always scrutinizing arguments, and refuses to be convinced straight away of whatever anyone says.'

Simmias said, 'Well, Socrates, this time, at least, I too think that there's something in what Cebes is saying. With what motive would truly wise men try to escape from masters better than themselves and give them up without a fight? And I think that Cebes is aiming his argument at you, because you are accepting without a fight your departure both from us and from those good rulers, as you yourself agree they are, the gods.'

63b 'What the two of you are saying is fair,' he said. 'I suppose you mean that I must defend myself in answer to these charges, as if in court.'

'That's quite right,' said Simmias.

'Very well then,' he said, 'let me attempt to defend myself more persuasively to you than I did to my jurors. Well, Simmias and Cebes,' he said, 'if I didn't think that I'll enter, firstly, the company of other gods, who are both wise and good, and secondly the company of humans who have died and who are better than the people here, then it would be wrong of me not to resent my death. As things stand, however, I assure you that I am hoping to join the company of good men. I wouldn't absolutely insist on this latter, but as for entering the company of gods who are entirely good masters, be sure that if there is anything of this sort that I *would* insist on it is on that. For these reasons I'm not as resentful as I'd otherwise be, but am optimistic that there is something in store for the dead and, as we have long been told, something much better for the good than for the bad.' 63c

'Well then, Socrates,' said Simmias. 'Do you intend to depart keeping this thought to yourself, or would you share it with us too? I think after all that this is a good in which we too have an interest. And at the same time, should you convince us of what you're saying, it will serve you as that defence.' 63d

'Of course, I'll try,' he said. 'But first let's deal with Crito here and see what it is that I think he's been wanting to say for quite some time.'

'Just this, Socrates,' said Crito. 'For some time the man who will give you the poison has been telling me that I must instruct you to keep the conversation as short as possible. He says this is because during conversation people get too hot, and one shouldn't combine any overheating with taking the poison. Otherwise, those who do so are sometimes forced to drink two or even three doses.' 63e

'Never mind him,' said Socrates. 'Just let him make arrangements for giving two doses, or even three, if need be.'

'Well, I pretty much knew you'd say this,' said Crito, 'but he's been pestering me for some time.'

'Don't mind him,' he said. 'But to *you*, my jurors, I want now to give the account I owe you, of how it seems to me to be reasonable for a man who has genuinely spent his life in philosophy to be confident about his imminent death, and to be optimistic that he'll win the greatest goods there, after he's met his end. So I'll try to explain, Simmias and Cebes, how this could be the case. 64a

'Well, other people have probably not realized that the sole pursuit of those who correctly engage in philosophy is dying and being dead. If this is true, it would surely be absurd for death to be their sole aim throughout their life, but, when it actually arrives, for them to resent that which has long been their aim and pursuit.'

64b   Simmias laughed at that. 'Indeed, Socrates,' he said, 'I was in absolutely no mood for laughing just then, but you made me do so. I think that most people, on hearing this point, would think it altogether well said about those who pursue philosophy – and people back home would agree entirely – that those who pursue philosophy really are near death,[13] and that they themselves have realized that death is just what these people deserve.'

'Yes, and they'd be telling the truth, Simmias, except when they say that they've realized it – because they haven't realized the *sense* in which true philosophers are near death, the sense in which they deserve death,

64c   and what that death is like. Let's speak,' he said, 'among ourselves and ignore them. Do we believe that there is such a thing as death?'

'Certainly,' replied Simmias.

'Can we believe that it is anything other than the separation of the soul from the body? And do we believe that being dead is the following: the body has been separated from the soul and come to be apart, alone by itself, and the soul has been separated from the body and is apart, alone by itself. Can death be anything other than that?'

'No, that's what it is,' he said.

64d   'Consider then, my friend, if you too turn out to think what I do. I believe that the following points will give us a better understanding of the things we are looking into. Does it seem to you in character for a philosophical man to be eager for such so-called pleasures as those of food and drink?'

'No, not at all, Socrates,' said Simmias.

'How about those of sex?'

'By no means.'

'What about the other sorts of attention given to the body? Do you think someone like that holds them in high regard? Take, for example, acquiring superior clothing and shoes and the other ways of adorning the

64e   body: do you think he values them, or attaches no value to them except in so far as he absolutely must take an interest in them?'

'No value, I think,' he said, 'at least if he's truly a philosopher.'

---

[13] The verb translated here and in the next paragraph as 'be near death' could also mean 'want to die'. But there is no such ambiguity at 65a6, where Socrates says that, according to most people, philosophers come 'pretty close to being dead'.

'In short, then, do you think,' he said, 'that such a man's concern is not for the body, and that, as far as he can, he stands apart from it and is turned towards his soul?'

'Yes, I do.'

'So first of all is it clear that in matters like these the philosopher   65a releases his soul as much as possible from its association with the body, he above all other people?'

'So it seems.'

'And ordinary people think, don't they, Simmias, that life isn't worth living for someone who finds nothing of that kind pleasant, and who takes no interest in bodily things. They think that he who gives no thought to the pleasures which come via the body is pretty close to being dead.'

'Yes, what you say is quite true.'

'What about the acquisition of wisdom itself? Is the body an imped- iment or not if one recruits it as a partner in one's inquiry? I mean   65b something like this: do both sight and hearing offer people any truth? Or are even the poets always telling us this sort of mantra, that nothing we hear or see is accurate? And yet if these particular bodily senses are not accurate or clear, then the *others* will hardly be, because, I assume, they are all inferior to them. Don't you think so?'

'Certainly.'

'So,' he said, 'when does the soul grasp the truth? Because whenever it attempts to examine something together with the body, clearly at those times it is thoroughly deceived by the body.'

'That is true.'   65c

'Then isn't it in reasoning – if anywhere – that the soul discovers something real?'

'Yes.'

'Right, and surely it reasons best when it is being troubled neither by hearing nor by sight nor by pain, nor by a certain sort of pleasure either, but when it as much as possible comes to be alone by itself, ignoring the body, and, as far as it can, doesn't associate or have contact with the body when reaching out to what is real.'

'That's true.'

'So here too does the philosopher's soul particularly devalue the body   65d and try to escape from it, seeking instead to become alone by itself?'

'So it seems.'

51

'And now what about things like the following, Simmias? Do we say that there is a Just itself or not?'

'Indeed we do!'

'Yes, and a Beautiful and a Good?'

'Of course.'

'Now have you ever actually seen with your eyes any of the things of this kind?'

'Not at all,' he said.

'Or have you grasped them with one of the other senses that operate through the body? I am talking about all of them, such as Largeness, Health, Strength[14] and, to sum up, about the being[15] of all the rest – what

65e   each of them really is. Are they viewed at their truest through the body, or is the following rather the case: that whichever of us trains himself most, and with the greatest precision, to think about each thing investigated as an object in its own right, *he* would come closest to knowing each of them?'

'Certainly.'

'So wouldn't the man who did this most purely be one who so far as possible used his thought in its own right to access each reality, neither

66a   adducing the evidence of his sight in his thinking nor bringing any other sense at all along with his reasoning, but using his thought alone by itself and unalloyed, and so attempting to hunt down each real thing alone by itself and unalloyed, separated as far as possible from eyes and ears and virtually from his entire body, for the reason that the body disturbs his soul and, whenever it associates with it, doesn't let it acquire truth and wisdom? Isn't this, Simmias, the man who will hit upon reality, if anyone will?'

'That's eminently true, Socrates,' said Simmias.

66b   'Then given all this,' he said, 'is it inevitable for those who are genuinely philosophers to be struck by the following sort of belief, so that they also tell one another things like this: "You know, a sort of short cut may well be taking us with our reason towards the quarry in our inquiry, because as long as we have the body and our soul is fused with bodily evil, we'll *never* properly acquire what we desire, namely, as we would say, the truth.

66c   For the body detains us in countless ways because of the sustenance it

---

[14] For this trio see also *Meno* 72d–e, a passage which suggests that they, unlike the preceding trio, are Forms that are already well understood and can therefore provide a model for investigating the Forms of values.

[15] See p. 3 n. 6.

needs. Besides, should certain diseases attack it, they impede our hunt for reality. The body fills us up with loves, desires, fears and fantasies of every kind, and a great deal of nonsense, with the result that it really and truly, as the saying goes, makes it impossible for us even to think about anything at any moment. For it is nothing but the body and its desires that causes wars, uprisings and conflicts. All wars arise for the sake of acquiring property, and we are compelled to acquire property on account 66d of the body, enslaved as we are to its maintenance. It is thanks to the body that, for all these reasons, we have no time for philosophy. Though the worst of all is that even if we do get some respite from the body and turn to pursuing some inquiry, in our investigations it yet again turns up everywhere, causes confusion and turmoil, and overwhelms us, so as to prevent us from being able to keep the truth in sight. But we really have shown that if we are ever to have pure knowledge of something, we must be separated from the body and view things by themselves with the soul 66e by itself. The time when we will have that which we desire and whose lovers we claim to be, namely wisdom, will be when we are dead, as the argument indicates, and not while we are alive. For if it is impossible to have pure knowledge of anything when we are in the company of the body, then either knowledge cannot be acquired anywhere, or it can be acquired when we are dead. For then the soul will be alone by itself, 67a apart from the body, whereas before then it will not. And in the time when we are alive, it seems that we will be closest to knowledge if, so far as possible, we have no dealings with the body and do not associate with it except when absolutely necessary, and are not infected with its nature, but instead keep pure from it, until the god himself releases us. If we stay pure in this way by being separated from the body's folly, in all likelihood we will be with people[16] of this kind, and will know through our very selves everything that is unalloyed, which is, equally, the truth. For it may 67b be that it is not sanctioned for someone impure to grasp something pure." I think these are the sort of things, Simmias, that all those who truly love learning must tell one another and believe. Or do you not think so?'

'I do, more than anything.'

'Then,' said Socrates, 'if all this is true, my friend, for someone who reaches the place to which I am journeying there is every hope that there, if anywhere, he will properly acquire that for the sake of which we have

---

[16] The Greek could also mean 'with *things* of this kind' (that is, with pure things).

67c worked hard in our past life. Hence the travel now assigned to me comes with good hope, as it does for any other man who considers his thought to have been purified, as it were, and so readied.'

'Certainly,' said Simmias.

'And doesn't purification turn out to be the very thing we were recently talking about in our discussion,[17] namely parting the soul from the body as much as possible and habituating it to assembling and gathering itself from every part of the body, alone by itself, and to living alone by itself as

67d far as it can, both now and afterwards, released from the body as if from fetters?'

'Certainly,' he said.

'So is it *this* that is named "death": release and parting of soul from body?'

'Yes, entirely so,' he said.

'Right, and according to us it is those who really love wisdom[18] who are always particularly eager – or rather, who *alone* are always eager – to release it, and philosophers' practice is just that, release and parting of soul from body. Or isn't it?'

'It seems to be.'

'So, just as I was saying at the beginning,[19] wouldn't it be laughable

67e for a man to be as close as possible to dead, and so to train himself to live like that, but then, when death comes to him, to resent it?'

'It would be laughable, of course.'

'In that case, Simmias,' he said, 'those who truly love wisdom are in reality practising dying, and being dead is least fearful to them of all people. Consider it in the following way. If they are at odds with the body in every respect, and desire to have the soul alone by itself, but were afraid and resentful when this actually happened, wouldn't that be extremely

68a irrational – if, that is, they did not go cheerfully to the place where, on their arrival, they hope to attain that with which they were in love throughout life, namely wisdom, and to be separated from the company of that with which they were at odds? When human boyfriends, wives and sons have died, very many people have readily consented to go after them into Hades, led by the hope that there they will see the people they

---

[17] At 64d–66a.
[18] *Philosophountes*, that is, those who are philosophers (*philosophoi*), which literally means 'lovers of wisdom'. The translation will vary between 'philosopher(s)' and 'lover(s) of wisdom'.
[19] At 64a.

longed for and be with them. Yet will someone who is genuinely in love with wisdom, and has strongly conceived this same hope that nowhere but in Hades will he have a worthwhile encounter with it, resent dying   68b and go there less than cheerfully? One can only think he will not, at least if he is *really* a lover of wisdom, my friend. For he will be quite sure that he will have a pure encounter with wisdom nowhere else but there. And if this is so, as I was just saying,[20] wouldn't it be extremely irrational if someone like that were to fear death?'

'Extremely irrational, indeed.'

'Then' he said, 'if you see that a man is resentful that he is about to die, is that sufficient proof for you that he was not a lover of wisdom but   68c a sort of body-lover? And this same man, I take it, is also a money-lover and honour-lover, either one of these or both.'

'It's entirely as you say,' he said.

'So, Simmias,' he said, 'doesn't that which is called "courage" also belong most to those with this attitude?'

'Quite so,' he said.

'And temperance as well – that which even ordinary people call "temperance", namely not being in a flutter about one's desires, but rather being disdainful towards them and staying composed – doesn't that belong only to those who particularly disdain the body and live in philosophy?'

'It must,' he said.   68d

'Right,' he said, 'because if you care to think about other people's courage and temperance, you'll find these to be absurd.'

'How so, Socrates?'

'Are you aware,' he said, 'that all those other people consider death to be one of the great evils?'

'Very much so,' he said.

'Then is it fear of greater evils that makes the brave among them endure death, whenever they do so?'

'That's right.'

'In that case it is being afraid and fear that make everyone except philosophers courageous. And yet it is unreasonable, to say the least, that fear and cowardice should make someone courageous.'

'Certainly.'   68e

[20] At 67e.

'What about those among them who keep their composure? Hasn't this same thing happened to them – it is a sort of intemperance that makes them temperate? And yet, although we *say* that it is impossible, all the same in their case what *happens* concerning that simple-minded temperance turns out to be like this: because they fear being denied other pleasures, which they desire, they abstain from one set of pleasures because they are overcome by another set of pleasures. Yet although they

69a *call* being ruled by their pleasures "intemperance", what actually happens is that they overcome some pleasures because they are overcome by other pleasures. And this resembles what we were just talking about – that it is in a way because of intemperance that they have become temperate.'

'Yes, it is similar.'

'For I suspect, my good Simmias, that for the purpose of virtue this is not the correct exchange, the exchanging of pleasures for pleasures, pains for pains and fear for fear, greater for less, like currencies, but that just one thing is the correct currency, in return for which one must

69b exchange all these: I mean wisdom. Now when all things are bought and sold for this and with this – with wisdom – they really are, I suspect, courage, temperance, justice and in sum true virtue, regardless of whether pleasures, fears and everything else like that are added or removed. But when they are kept apart from wisdom and exchanged for one another, that sort of virtue is, I fear, a kind of illusion: it is really fit for slaves, and

69c contains nothing sound or true. The reality is, I suspect, that temperance, justice and courage are a kind of purification from everything like this, and that wisdom itself is a kind of rite to purify us. So it actually seems that those people who established the rites for us are no ordinary people, but in reality have long been setting a riddle when they say that whoever comes to Hades without initiation and the rites will lie in filth, whereas someone who arrives there purified and initiated will dwell with gods. For

69d in fact, as those involved in the rites put it, "many carry the fennel-wand, but few are inspired". The latter, in my opinion, are none other than those who have pursued philosophy correctly. In trying to become one of them I left nothing undone in my life, at least as far as I could, but did my utmost in every way. Whether I did so correctly and achieved anything, I'll know for certain when I've got there, god willing, and I don't think it will be long. This, then,' he said, 'Simmias and Cebes, is what I say in my defence to show that it is reasonable for me not to be upset or resentful

at leaving you and my masters here, as I believe that there too, no less   69e
than here, I'll meet good masters and companions. So if you find me any
more persuasive in my defence than the Athenians' jury did, that would
be welcome.'

When Socrates had said this, Cebes took up the conversation and
said: 'Socrates, I approve of the other things you say, but the matter   70a
of the soul causes people to have strong doubts and to worry that once
separated from the body it no longer exists anywhere, but is destroyed
and perishes on the day when the human being dies, immediately as it is
being separated from the body, and that as it comes out it is dissipated like
breath or smoke, flies away in all directions, and isn't anything anywhere.
For if it really *did* exist somewhere alone by itself, gathered together and
separated from these evils you just described, then there would be much   70b
hope, and a noble hope at that, Socrates, that what you say is true. But
this very point doubtless requires no little reassurance and proof, that
the soul exists when the human being has died, and has some power and
wisdom.'

'What you say is true, Cebes,' said Socrates. 'But what shall we do?
Would you like us to spend our conversation on these very questions, and
discuss whether or not it's likely to be so?'

'For my part,' said Cebes, 'I'd be glad to hear your view about them.'

'Anyhow, I really don't think,' said Socrates, 'that anyone who heard   70c
us now, even if he were a comic poet,[21] would say that I'm prattling on
and talking about irrelevant things. If that's the decision, then, we should
consider it thoroughly.

'Let's consider it in the following sort of way. Let's see whether or
not it turns out that when people have died their souls exist in Hades.
Now there is an ancient saying which comes to mind, that souls exist
there when they have come from here, and that they come back here and
come to be[22] from dead people. If this is so – that living people come
to be again from those who have died – surely our souls would exist   70d
there? For, I take it, the souls would not come to be again, if they did not
exist. And so it would be evidence enough of the truth of this, should it

---

[21] A reference to Aristophanes, who in *Clouds* 1485 describes Socrates and Socrates' students as 'prattlers'.
[22] That is, come to be the souls of living people. The verb translated as 'come to be' can also mean 'be born', and it is translated as such during the Recollection argument (73a–77a). But in this passage, as in 77c–d, Socrates is arguing from a general principle about how things *come to be* F.

really come to be clear that living people come to be from nowhere other than from the dead. But if this is not true, we would need some other argument.'

'Quite so,' said Cebes.

'Well then,' he said, 'if you want to understand more easily, don't consider this with regard to humans only, but in relation to all animals and plants too. In short, concerning everything that has a coming-to-be,

70e let us see whether they all come to be in this way: the opposites from nowhere other than their opposites – all those, that is, that actually have an opposite, as for example the beautiful is surely opposite to the ugly, and just to unjust, and there are countless others like this. So let's consider whether everything that has an opposite necessarily comes to be from nowhere other than from its opposite. For example, whenever something comes to be larger, I presume that it is necessarily from being smaller before that the thing later comes to be larger?'

'Yes.'

71a 'Also, if it comes to be smaller, is it from being larger before that it will later come to be smaller?'

'That's so,' he said.

'Again, is it from being stronger that the weaker comes to be, and from slower the faster?'

'Certainly.'

'Well, if something comes to be worse, won't it do so from better, and if more just, from more unjust?'

'Of course.'

'So,' he said, 'we have a satisfactory grasp of this: all opposite things come to be in this way, from opposites?'

'Certainly.'

'Next, is there something of the following kind too found in them? Between all the pairs of opposites – two in each case – are there two pro-

71b cesses of coming-to-be, from the first to the second and conversely from the second to the first? Between a thing when greater and smaller are there increase and decrease, and do we accordingly call the one "increasing", the other "decreasing"?'

'Yes,' he said.

'And again "detaching" and "combining", "cooling" and "heating", and so on. Even if we don't use names for them in some cases, still in point of fact mustn't the following be true in every case, namely that they come to be from one another and that there is a process of coming-to-be of each into the other?'

'Yes indeed,' he said.

'Very well,' he said. 'Is there an opposite to living, as sleeping is to being awake?' 71c

'There certainly is,' he said.

'What is it?'

'Being dead,' he said.

'Then do these come to be from one another, given that they are opposites,[23] and are the processes of coming-to-be between them two in number, as they themselves are two?'

'Of course.'

'Well then,' said Socrates, 'I'll tell you one of the pairs I just mentioned, both the pair itself and its processes of coming-to-be, and you tell me the other pair. I call one thing "being asleep", another "being awake", and say that it is from being asleep that being awake comes to be, and from 71d being awake being asleep, and that their processes of coming-to-be are falling asleep and waking up. Does that satisfy you,' he said, 'or not?'

'Certainly.'

'Now *you* tell me,' he said, 'about life and death in the same way. Don't you say that being dead is the opposite of being alive?'

'I do.'

'And that they come to be from one another?'

'Yes.'

'So what is it that comes to be from that which is living?'

'That which is dead,' he said.

'And what,' he said, 'from that which is dead?'

'I must grant,' he said, 'that it's that which is living.'

'In that case, Cebes, is it from those that are dead that both living things and living people come to be?'

'It appears so,' he said. 71e

'Then our souls exist in Hades,' he said.

'So it seems.'

'Now as for their two processes of coming-to-be, is there one, at any rate, that is in fact unmistakable? I mean dying is unmistakable, isn't it?'

'Certainly,' said Cebes.

---

[23] The translation '*if* they are opposites' is also possible.

'So what will we do?' said Socrates. 'Will we refuse to balance it with the opposite process of coming-to-be, and instead will nature be handicapped in this respect? Or must we balance dying with an opposite process of coming-to-be?'

'I suppose we must,' he said.

'And what will this be?'

'Returning to life.'

'So,' he said, 'if there is such a thing as returning to life, would this 72a – returning to life – be a process of coming-to-be from dead people to living ones?'

'Certainly.'

'In that case, we agree in this way too that living people have come to be from the dead no less than dead people from the living. And we thought, I take it, that if this were true there would be sufficient evidence that the souls of the dead must exist somewhere, and that it is from there that they come to be again.'

'Given what we agreed, Socrates,' he said, 'I think this must be so.'

'Well then, Cebes,' he said, 'here is a way for you to see that we aren't wrong in what we have agreed, or so I think. Suppose the one set of 72b things did not always balance the other by coming to be, going round in a circle, as it were, but instead the process of coming-to-be were a straight line from the one to its opposite only, and did not bend back again to the former or turn in its course. Do you realize that then everything in the end would have the same form, be in the same condition, and stop coming to be?'

'What do you mean?' said Cebes.

'It's not hard,' said Socrates, 'to get an idea of what I'm talking about. For example, if there were falling asleep, but waking up did not balance it 72c by coming to be from the sleeping, do you realize that the eventual state of things would make Endymion[24] look insignificant: he would go quite unnoticed, because everything else too would have fallen into the same condition as his – sleeping. Also, if everything underwent combining, but not detaching, soon Anaxagoras' saying would have come true: "all things together".[25] In the same way too, my dear Cebes, if everything that

---

[24] In Greek myth, an outstandingly beautiful youth who was kept that way by being given eternal sleep.

[25] The treatise of Anaxagoras of Clazomenae (*c.* 500–428 BC; see further at 97b–99c) began 'All things were together.'

partook in living were to die, and if, when they had died, the dead were
to remain in that form and not return to life, wouldn't it be absolutely
unavoidable for everything in the end to be dead and nothing alive? For   72d
if living things came to be from the other things, and if the living things
died, how could they be prevented from all being expended and ending
up dead?'

'I think that would be inevitable, Socrates,' said Cebes, 'and in my
opinion what you're saying is completely true.'

'Yes, Cebes,' he said, 'I think that is exactly how it is. And we're not
deluded in agreeing to this precise account, but these are all facts: coming
back to life, living people coming to be from the dead, the souls of the dead
existing, and its being better for good souls and worse for bad ones.'[26]

'Besides, Socrates,' replied Cebes, 'also according to that theory which   72e
you yourself habitually propound, that our learning is in fact nothing but
recollection, according to it too, if it's true, we must presumably have
learned in some previous time what we recollect now. And that would be   73a
impossible if our soul did not exist somewhere before it was born in this
human form. So in this way too the soul seems to be something immortal.'

'But Cebes,' Simmias replied, 'what are the proofs for this? Remind
me, because I don't quite remember at the moment.'

'It's shown,' said Cebes, 'by one particularly fine argument: when people are questioned, provided someone questions them well, they themselves come up with true statements about everything. And yet they
wouldn't be able to do so, if knowledge and a correct account were not
actually inside them. For example, if one confronts them with diagrams   73b
or something else of the kind, that is the situation in which one shows
most clearly that this is the case.'[27]

'And if you aren't convinced in this way, Simmias,' said Socrates, 'see
if you agree when you examine the issue along the following lines. For
are you in doubt about how so-called "learning" can be recollection?'

'No, I don't doubt it,' said Simmias, 'but I need to undergo the very
thing that the theory is about: recollecting. And to *some* extent I already
remember and am convinced, thanks to what Cebes started to say. None

---

[26] The words translated 'and its being better for good souls and worse for bad ones', although present
in the manuscripts, are omitted from most modern editions as an insertion from 63c6–7. But if
they are retained, each of the three stages of the Cyclical Argument (71e, 72a, 72d) concludes with
a differently worded vindication of the Hades tradition, which at 70c–d the argument set out to
prove.
[27] A clear reference to *Meno* 81a–86c.

the less, I'd like to hear now how you yourself were starting to propound it.'

73c   'It was as follows,' he said. 'We agree, I take it, that if someone is going to recollect something, he must know it at some earlier time.'

'Certainly.'

'Now do we also agree that whenever knowledge comes in the following sort of way, it is recollection? What way do I mean? I'll tell you. Suppose someone sees or hears or has some other perception of one thing, and not only recognizes that thing, but also comes to think of something else which is the object not of the same knowledge but of a different one: aren't we right to say that he recollected this second thing, the one of
73d   which he had the thought?'

'What do you mean?'

'I mean things of this kind: knowledge of a person is, I suppose, different from knowledge of a lyre?'

'Of course.'

'Now are you aware that whenever lovers see a lyre or cloak or something else that their boyfriends use regularly, they have the following experience: don't they both recognize the lyre, and come to have in their thinking the appearance of the boy whose lyre it is? This is recollection. Exactly, in fact, as someone upon seeing Simmias often recollects Cebes – and I imagine there'd be countless other cases of this kind.'

'Countless indeed,' said Simmias.

73e   'Well then,' he said, 'is that sort of thing a kind of recollection? And above all whenever someone has undergone this experience concerning things which he had by now forgotten because of the length of time in which he has not turned his mind to them?'

'Certainly,' he said.

'Very well,' said he. 'Can it happen that upon seeing a painting of a horse or lyre one recollects a person; and upon seeing a painting of Simmias one recollects Cebes?'

'Yes indeed.'

'And also that upon seeing a painting of Simmias one recollects Simmias himself?'

74a   'That certainly can happen,' he said.

'So, in view of all these, doesn't it follow that recollection happens from similar things, but happens from dissimilar things too?'

'Yes, it does follow.'

'But whenever it is from *similar* things that one recollects something, is it not true that one inevitably has the following experience as well: that of thinking whether or not in its similarity it in some way falls short of the thing one has recollected?'

'Yes, inevitably,' he said.

'Consider then,' said he, 'if this is the case. We say, I take it, that there is an Equal – I don't mean a stick equal to another stick, or a stone equal to a stone, or anything else of the kind, but something else besides all these, the Equal itself. Should we say that there is such a thing or not?'

'Indeed we should,' said Simmias, 'emphatically so!' 74b

'Do we also know what it is?'

'Certainly,' he said.

'Having got the knowledge of it from where? Wasn't it from the things we were just mentioning? Upon seeing that either sticks or stones or some other things were equal, wasn't it from them that we came to think of it, different as it is from them? Or doesn't it appear different to you? Consider it in this way as well. Don't equal stones and sticks some-times, despite being the same ones, appear at one time equal, at another not?'[28]

'Certainly.'

'Well, have the Equals themselves ever appeared to you unequal, or 74c has equality ever appeared as inequality?'

'No, not yet at any rate, Socrates.'

'In that case,' he said, 'these equal things and the Equal itself are not the same thing.'

'Not at all, Socrates, by the look of things.'

'But still,' he said, 'it's from these equal things, though they are dif-ferent from that Equal, that you have nonetheless thought of and got the knowledge of it?'

'Very true,' said Simmias.

'Now it is either similar to them or dissimilar, isn't it?'

'Certainly.'

---

[28] An alternative manuscript tradition, followed by many editors and translators, gives 'Don't equal stones and sticks sometimes, despite being the same, appear equal to one, but not to another?' Those who render it this way are divided as to whether 'to one . . . to another' refers to people, and is to be construed with 'appear', or to stones and sticks, and is to be construed with 'equal'. For defence of the reading followed here see David Sedley, 'Equal sticks and stones' in D. Scott (ed.), *Maieusis: Essays in Ancient Philosophy in Honour of Myles Burnyeat* (Oxford, 2007), 68–86. Cf. also p. xxx.

'Yes, but it makes no difference,' he said. 'So long as upon seeing one
74d thing you come from this sight to think of something else, whether similar
or dissimilar, it must,' he said, 'have been recollection.'

'Quite so.'

'Well then,' he said, 'do we experience something like the following
as regards what happens in the case of sticks and, more generally, the
equal things we just mentioned? Do they seem to us to be equal in the
same manner as what Equal itself is? Alternatively, do they in some
way fall short of it when it comes to being like the Equal? Or in no
way?'

'They fall *far* short,' said Simmias.

'Now do we agree that whenever someone, upon seeing something,
74e thinks "What I am now seeing wants to be like some other real thing, but
falls short and can't be like it, and instead is inferior", the person who
thinks this must presumably have actually known beforehand the thing
he says it resembles but falls short of?'

'Yes, he must.'

'Very well. Have we too experienced something like that, or not, concerning equal things and the Equal itself?'

'Definitely.'

75a 'In that case, we must have known the Equal before the time when we
first, upon seeing equal things, came to think: "All these are seeking to
be like the Equal, but fall short of it."'

'That's true.'

'Now we also agree that we haven't come to think of it, and indeed can't
come to think of it, from anywhere other than from seeing or touching or
from some other sense – I count them all as the same.'

'Yes, because they are the same, Socrates, at least in relation to what
the argument aims to show.'

'Now then, it is from the senses that one must come to think that
75b everything in the reach of the senses both seeks that thing which Equal
is and falls short of it. What do we say?'

'Just that.'

'Then before we started to see and hear and use the other senses,
presumably we must in fact have got knowledge of what the Equal itself
is, if we were going to refer to it the equal things deriving from the senses,
saying they all are eager to be like it, but are inferior to it.'

'Necessarily, given what has already been said, Socrates.'

'Now was it from the moment we were born that we started seeing and hearing and having use of the other senses?'

'Certainly.'

'Right, and we must, as we're saying, have got the knowledge of the Equal before these?' 75c

'Yes.'

'In that case, it seems we must have got it before we were born.'

'Yes, so it seems.'

'Now if having got it before we were born, we were born with it in our grasp, did we know both before birth and from the moment we were born not only the Equal, the Larger, and the Smaller, but also the entire set of such things? For our present argument is no more about the Equal than about the Beautiful itself, the Good itself, the Just, the Pious, and, 75d as I've been saying, about everything to which we attach this label, "what such and such is",[29] both when asking our questions and when giving our answers. So we must have got the knowledge of each of these before we were born.'

'That's true.'

'And if after getting it we have not forgotten them each time, we must always be born knowing and must know at all times throughout our life. For this is knowing: having got knowledge of something, to hold it in one's grasp and not have lost it. Or isn't it loss of knowledge that we call forgetting, Simmias?'

'Certainly, Socrates,' he said. 75e

'On the other hand, I think, if having got it before birth we lost it in the course of being born, but later by using our senses we started regaining those items of knowledge about them which at an earlier time we had in our grasp, wouldn't what we call "learning" be regaining our own knowledge? And surely we'd be right to call this "recollecting"?'

'Definitely.'

'Right, because this was shown to be possible: upon perceiving some- 76a thing – whether by seeing or hearing, or by getting some other perception of it – thanks to it, to come to think of something else which one had forgotten, something with which the first thing, though dissimilar, had a connection, or something to which it was similar. And so, just as I've

---

[29] For this and similar locutions for Forms, compare 65d–e, 74d, 75b, 78d, 92e; *Symposium* 211c–d; *Republic* 490b, 507b, 532a–b.

been saying, one of these two must be true: either all of us have been born knowing them and have lifelong knowledge of them, or the people we describe as "learning" simply recollect at a later stage, and learning would be recollection.'

'Exactly so, Socrates.'

76b 'Which then do you choose, Simmias? That we have been born knowing, or that we recollect later the things we had got knowledge of before?'

'Right now, Socrates, I'm unable to choose between them.'

'Well can you make *this* choice, and what do you think about it? If a man has knowledge, could he or couldn't he give an account of what he knows?'

'He must be able to, Socrates,' he said.

'And do you really think that everyone can give an account of the things we just mentioned?'

'I'd certainly like that to be true,' said Simmias. 'But I'm far more afraid that this time tomorrow there will no longer be a single human being who can do this properly.'

76c 'In that case, Simmias,' he said, 'you don't think that everyone *knows* them.'

'Not at all.'

'Do they then recollect what they once learned?'

'Necessarily.'

'And when did our souls get the knowledge of them? It wasn't of course after we were born as human beings.'

'Certainly not.'

'Then it was earlier.'

'Yes.'

'In that case, Simmias, our souls existed earlier as well, separate from bodies, before they were in human form, and they had wisdom.'

'Unless, perhaps, we get these items of knowledge at the time when we are being born, Socrates – that time is still left.'

76d 'Well, my friend, in what other time do we lose them? Because of course we are not born with them in our grasp, as we just agreed. Or do we lose them at the very time when we get them? Or can you tell me some other time?'

'Not at all, Socrates – I didn't notice that there was nothing in what I was saying.'

'So is this how the facts stand for us, Simmias?' he said. 'If the things which are our constant refrain really exist, I mean a Beautiful and a Good and all that sort of being, and if we refer to this being everything derived from our senses, rediscovering our ownership of what belonged to us before, and compare them to it, then just as *these* things exist, so too must our soul also exist even before we are born. But if they don't exist, then wouldn't this argument turn out to have been propounded to no effect? Is that right, and is it equally necessary that they exist and that our souls existed before *we* were born, and if the former is not necessary, then the latter is not either?'[30] 76e

'I'm extremely sure, Socrates,' said Simmias, 'that there is the same necessity, and it is to our advantage that the argument resorts to the point 77a
that it is as certain that our soul existed before our birth as that the being you mention now exists. For I have nothing that is as clear to me as that there exists, as much as anything could exist, everything of this sort, Beautiful, Good and all the other things you just mentioned. And at least in my opinion it has been sufficiently proved.'

'But what about Cebes?' said Socrates. 'We must of course convince Cebes too.'

'It's been proved sufficiently for him,' said Simmias, 'at least in my view, though he's more resolute than anyone in not believing arguments. All the same, I imagine he's been fully convinced that our soul existed before we were born. But whether it will still exist when we've died as 77b
well, that doesn't seem, even to me, to have been proved, Socrates,' he said. 'What Cebes recently said[31] still stands in our way, the common fear that at the time when the human being dies his or her soul is dissipated and this is the end of its existence. For why shouldn't it be that, on the one hand, the soul is born and constituted from somewhere else, and exists before it ever enters a human body, but that, on the other hand, when the soul has entered a body, and is being separated from it, it itself then dies and is destroyed?'

'Well said, Simmias,' said Cebes. 'For it appears that half of what is 77c
needed has been proved, namely that our soul existed before our birth.

[30] The Greek here more literally means 'and if not the one, not the other either'. This is usually expanded into 'And if the former do not exist, the latter did not either', but our expansion into 'if the former is not necessary, then the latter is not either' seems required by the logic of the passage.
[31] At 70a.

We must also prove that when we have died it will exist no less than it did before our birth, if the proof is to be complete.'

'It has already been shown, Simmias and Cebes,' said Socrates, 'if you're prepared to combine this argument with the one we agreed to before it – that everything living comes to be from what is dead. For if 77d the soul exists before as well, and if, when it enters upon living and comes to be, it must do so from nowhere other than from death and from being dead, surely it must exist also when it has died, simply because it has to come to be again?

'So what you both mention has been proved already. But none the less I think that both you and Simmias would gladly persevere with this argument too even more thoroughly, and that you fear what children fear – namely that what really happens is that when the soul leaves the 77e body the wind blows it apart and dissipates it, especially when someone happens to die not in calm weather but in a strong wind.'

Cebes laughed at that. 'Try to convince us, Socrates,' he said, 'as if we do have that fear. Or rather, not as if *we* have the fear – maybe there's a child actually inside us who's afraid of things like that. So try to convince that child to stop fearing death as if it were the bogeyman.'

'Well,' said Socrates, 'you must chant spells to him every day until you manage to chant it away.'

78a 'Where then, Socrates,' he said, 'will we find a good enchanter for such things, given that you,' he added, 'are leaving us?'

'Greece is a large place, Cebes,' he said, 'and there are no doubt good men in it. There are also many races of foreigners. All of these people you must comb in your search for such an enchanter, sparing neither money nor effort, as there's nothing on which you'd be better off spending money. But you must yourselves work together as you search, because you may not easily find others more able to do this than you.'

78b 'Yes, that will be done,' said Cebes. 'But let's return to where we left off, if that's to your liking.'

'It certainly is. How wouldn't it be?'

'Excellent,' he said.

'Well then,' said Socrates, 'should we ask ourselves a question along the following lines? What kind of thing is liable to undergo this – that is, to be dissipated? What kind of thing, I mean, is such that we should fear that it will be dissipated, and what kind of thing is not like that? And should we then consider to which of the two kinds soul belongs, and on that basis be confident or fearful on behalf of our own soul?'

'You're right,' he said.

'Now is it correct to say that what has been put together and is naturally 78c composite is the sort to be divided in the respect in which it was put together; and, on the other hand, that if something is actually incomposite, then it alone (if anything is) is the sort to escape division?'

'Yes, I think that's so,' said Cebes.

'Now isn't it true that the things that are always in the same state and condition are most likely to be the incomposite ones, whereas those that are in different conditions at different times and are never in the same state are most likely to be composite?'

'I think so.'

'Then let's turn,' he said, 'to the same things as in the previous argument. Take the essential being which is the object of our account 78d when in our questions and answers we explain *what it is*. Does it always stay in the same condition and state, or is it in different conditions at different times? The Equal itself, the Beautiful itself, what each thing itself is, that which really is – is that ever subject to change of any kind at all? Or does *what each of them is* always stay in the same condition and state, uniform and alone by itself, and never in any respect or manner subject to any alteration?'

'It must stay in the same condition and state, Socrates,' said Cebes.

'What about the many beautiful things, such as people or horses or cloaks or any other things whatsoever that have that particular property? 78e Or again, things that are equal, and so on for all the things that share the names of those entities we mentioned? Do they stay in the same state, or, in quite the opposite way to those entities, are they virtually never in the same state at all, either as themselves or as one another?'

'They too,' said Cebes, 'are as you say: they never stay in the same condition.'

'Now isn't it true that these you could touch, see and perceive with the 79a other senses, but that when it comes to those that stay in the same state, you could never get hold of them with anything other than the reasoning of your thought, such things being unseen and not visible?'

'That's absolutely true,' said Cebes.

'So do you want us to assume,' said Socrates, 'that there are two classes of beings, one visible, the other unseen?'

'Let's do so,' he said.

'The unseen always staying in the same state, the visible never doing so?'

'Let's assume that too,' he said.

79b   'Now,' he said, 'aren't we ourselves part soul, part body?'

'Exactly so,' he said.

'Then to which of the two sorts do we say the body would be more similar and more akin?'

'That much,' he said, 'is obvious to everyone: to the visible.'

'What about the soul? Is it something visible or unseen?'

'It isn't seen by human beings, at any rate, Socrates,' he said.

'But what we were talking about was what is and what isn't visible to human nature. Or do you think that it was to some other nature?'

'No, to human nature.'

'So what do we say about soul? That it's visible or invisible?'

'Not visible.'

'Unseen, then?'

'Yes.'

'In that case, soul is more similar than body to the unseen, whereas body is more similar to the visible.'

79c   'That's absolutely inevitable, Socrates.'

'Now weren't we also saying some time ago[32] that whenever the soul additionally uses the body for considering something, whether through seeing or through hearing or through some other sense – for to consider something through the body *is* to do so through sense-perception – at those times it is dragged by the body into things that never stay in the same state, and the soul itself wanders and is disturbed and giddy as if drunk, because the things it is grasping have the same kind of instability?'

'Certainly.'

79d   'But that whenever the soul considers alone by itself, it gets away into that which is pure, always in existence, and immortal, and which stays in the same condition; that the soul, because it is akin to this, always comes to be with it whenever alone by itself and able to do so; that the soul is then at rest from its wandering, and in relation to those entities stays always in the same state and condition, because the things it is grasping have the same kind of stability; and that this state of the soul is called "wisdom"?'

---

[32] At 65a–67b.

70

'That's completely right and true, Socrates,' he said.

'So, once again, given both what was said before and what we're saying now, to which of the two sorts do you think soul is more similar and more akin?'

79e

'I think, Socrates,' he said, 'that from this approach everyone, even the dullest learner, would grant that soul is in every possible way more similar to what always stays in the same condition than to what does not.'

'What about the body?'

'To the other sort.'

'Consider it along the following lines as well. Whenever soul and body are in the same place, nature instructs the latter to play the slave and be ruled, the former to rule and play the master. Again on this basis, which of the two do you think is similar to the divine, and which to the mortal? Or don't you think that the divine is naturally the kind to rule and lead, the mortal the kind to be ruled and play the slave?'

80a

'Yes, I do.'

'So which of the two does the soul resemble?'

'It's perfectly obvious, Socrates, that the soul resembles the divine, and that the body resembles the mortal.'

'Consider then, Cebes,' he said, 'whether from everything that has been said our results are as follows: that soul is most similar to that which is divine, immortal, intelligible, uniform, and incapable of being disintegrated, and which always stays in the same condition and state as itself; but that body, on the other hand, is most similar to what is human, mortal, resistant to intelligence, multiform, able to be disintegrated, and never in the same state as itself. Besides these properties, my dear Cebes, can we name any other in respect of which it does not turn out in this same way?'

80b

'No, we can't.'

'Very well. If all this is the case, isn't body the sort of thing to be quickly disintegrated, but soul, on the other hand, the sort to be altogether incapable of being disintegrated, or nearly so?'

'Yes, of course.'

80c

'Now do you realize,' he said, 'that when the human being has died, the visible part of him – the body, lodged in the visible realm, the thing that we call a corpse – which is the sort of thing to be disintegrated, fall apart and be scattered to the winds, does not find itself in any of these states straight away, but stays on for a reasonably long time, particularly if someone dies with his body in fine condition and at an age to match. For if the body has been shrunk and embalmed, like those who were 80d embalmed in Egypt, then it stays almost whole for an unimaginably long time, and even if the body rots, certain parts of it – bones, sinews and all such things – are still practically immortal, aren't they?'

'Yes.'

'But as for the soul, his unseen part, which gets away into a different place of this same kind, one which is noble, pure and unseen, Hades as it truly is,[33] where it will meet the good and wise god, the place to which, god willing, my soul too must go imminently – when the soul, which we have found to be naturally of this kind, is separated from the body, does it immediately get scattered to the winds[34] and perish, as ordinary 80e people say? Far from it, my dear Cebes and Simmias. Rather, the truth is as follows. First, take a case where a soul is separated in a pure condition, bringing with it nothing from the body, because it did not associate with the body at all in its life, at least when it had the choice, but instead avoided the body and stayed gathered together alone into itself, since that was its constant practice. Such a soul is doing nothing but pursue 81a philosophy correctly and practise to be ready for really being dead. Or wouldn't this be practice for death?'

'It certainly would.'

'So does a soul in this condition go off into what is similar to it, the unseen, the divine, immortal and wise, where after its arrival it can be happy, separated from wandering, unintelligence, fears, savage sorts of love and the other human evils, and just as is said of the initiates, does it truly spend the rest of time with gods? Is this what we should say, Cebes, or something else?'

'We should indeed say this,' replied Cebes.

81b 'But now, I mean, take a case where a soul has been defiled and is impure when it is separated from the body, because it has always been coupled[35] with the body, waited on it, loved it and been bewitched by it – by its desires and pleasures – so that the soul thinks nothing is real except the corporeal, what one can touch, see, drink, eat and enjoy sexually. On the other hand, it has come always to hate, dread and avoid what is murky

---

[33] Socrates exploits the similarity between 'Hades' (Greek *Haïdēs*) and *aïdēs* ('unseen'). At *Cratylus* 404b, however, Socrates rejects this as an actual etymology of the name.

[34] Compare 77e.

[35] The Greek verb (literally 'be with') is also used of sexual intercourse.

and unseen to the eyes, but is intelligible and is grasped with philosophy. Do you think that a soul in this condition will be unalloyed and alone by itself when separated?' 81c

'Certainly not,' he said.

'Instead, I suppose, it will be intermingled with the corporeal, which the body's company and coupling have made part of its nature, because of their constant coupling and because of its long practice?'

'That's right.'

'And one must suppose, my friend, that the corporeal is heavy, weighty, earthy and visible. That's what this sort of soul actually contains, and so it is weighed down and drawn back into the visible region by fear of the unseen and of Hades,[36] drifting, as it is said, around monuments and 81d tombs, the very places where certain shadowy apparitions of souls really have been seen. Such apparitions are presented by souls like these, those that have not been released in a pure way but have something of the visible – which is why they are seen.'

'Yes, that's likely, Socrates.'

'It certainly is likely, Cebes, and also that they are not at all the souls of the good, but those of the bad, which must wander around such places, paying the penalty for their former way of life, wicked as it was. What is more, they wander until the time when they are bound again into a body 81e by their desire for the corporeality that follows them around. And they are bound, in all likelihood, into whatever sorts of character they happen to have practised in their life.'

'Just which sorts do you mean, Socrates?'

'For example, it is likely that people who have practised acts of gluttony, recklessness and drunkenness, and have not shown caution, come to be embodied in the species which include donkeys and beasts like that. Don't 82a you think so?'

'That's very likely.'

'Right, and that those who have honoured, above all else, acts of injustice, tyrannies and thefts, are embodied in those species that include wolves, hawks and kites. Where else shall we say such souls would go?'

'No doubt,' said Cebes, 'into species like these.'

'Then,' he said, 'isn't it quite clear which way each of the other types too would go, on the basis of resemblance to their respective practices?'

---

[36] See n. 33 above.

'It's quite clear, of course,' he said.

82b 'Now are the happiest,' he said, 'even of these, and the ones that go to the best place, those who have pursued the common virtue of ordinary civic life, what they call "temperance" and "justice", which has come about from habit and practice without philosophy and intelligence?'

'In just what sense are these people happiest?'

'Because it's likely that they come back into a civic and tame species like themselves, that of bees, I suppose, or wasps or ants, or even back into the very same one, the human race, and that decent men are born from them.'

'That's likely.'

82c 'Yes, but coming into the race of gods is not sanctioned for anyone who did not pursue philosophy and has not departed in a perfectly pure condition, but only for one who loves learning. It is for these reasons, my dear Simmias and Cebes, that those who truly love wisdom keep away from all the desires that concern the body, retain their resolve, and do not surrender themselves to these desires, and not at all because they fear poverty and loss of property, as the money-loving majority do. Nor do they keep away from such desires because they fear dishonour and a reputation for immorality, as the lovers of power and honour do.'

'No, because that would be out of character, Socrates,' said Cebes.

82d 'Indeed it would,' he said. 'Because of this, Cebes, those who care at all about their own soul, and do not spend their lives getting their bodies into shape, dismiss all those people and do not take the same journey as they do, because they recognize that such people do not know where they are going. They themselves believe that in their actions they must not oppose philosophy and the release and purifying rite that philosophy provides. Following philosophy they head in the direction in which it leads.'

'How, Socrates?'

'I'll tell you,' he said. 'You see,' he continued, 'the lovers of learning 82e are aware that when philosophy takes over their soul, the soul really is bound thoroughly in the body and stuck to it, and is forced to consider the real things through it as if through a cage, and not on its own through itself, and that it drifts in utter ignorance. And philosophy observes the cleverness of the prison – that it works through desire, the best way to make the prisoner himself assist in his imprisonment. Anyway, as I was

saying, the lovers of learning are aware that the soul is in this condition   83a
when philosophy takes it over, and that philosophy gently reassures it
and attempts to release it by showing that inquiry conducted through the
eyes is full of deceit, as is likewise inquiry conducted through the ears and
through the other senses. Philosophy, they are aware, persuades the soul
to distance itself from the senses, except to the extent that use of them is
necessary, and encourages the soul to collect and gather itself alone into
itself, and to trust nothing but itself, concerning whichever real thing,   83b
alone by itself, the soul has intelligence of, when the soul too is alone by
itself. Philosophy, they are also aware, encourages the soul not to regard
as true anything else that the soul considers by other means and in other
things, and to believe that, whereas this latter kind of thing is perceptible
and visible, what the soul itself sees is intelligible and unseen.

'Now the soul of the true philosopher thinks that it should not oppose
this release, and that is why it refrains from pleasures, desires, pains and
fears as much as it can: it reckons that when someone experiences intense
pleasure, pain, fear or desire, they do not inflict on him the minor injuries
one might assume (for example, falling ill or wasting money because of   83c
his desires) but that they inflict on him the greatest and most extreme of
all evils, without it even appearing in his reckoning.'

'What is that, Socrates?' said Cebes.

'It's that the soul of every human being, when it experiences intense
pleasure or pain at something, is forced to believe at that moment that
whatever particularly gives rise to that feeling is most self-evidently real,
when it isn't so. These are above all visible things, aren't they?'

'Certainly.'

'Now is it when feeling this that soul is particularly bound tight by   83d
body?'

'How so?'

'Because each pleasure and pain rivets and pins it to the body as if with
a nail, and makes it corporeal, since it believes to be real the very things
that the body says are real. Since it has the same beliefs as the body and
enjoys the same things, it is forced, I think, to come to have the same ways
and the same sustenance, and to be the sort of soul never to enter Hades
in a pure condition, but every time to depart infected by the body, and so
to fall quickly back again into another body and, as it were, be sown and   83e
implanted, and because of this be deprived of the company of the divine
and pure and uniform.'

'That's very true, Socrates,' said Cebes.

'So, Cebes, it is for these reasons that the proper lovers of learning are composed and courageous. It is not for the reasons for which most people are so. Or do you think it is?'

84a 'No, I certainly don't.'

'No, indeed. But that is how a philosophical man's soul would reason. It would not suppose that, its own release being a job for philosophy, while philosophy is doing that the soul should of its own accord surrender itself for the pleasures and pains to bind it back inside again, and should undertake a Penelope's interminable task by working at a sort of web in reverse.[37] Instead such a man's soul secures a rest from these things, following its reasoning and being always engaged in reasoning, viewing

84b what is true, divine and not an object of opinion, and sustained by that, and supposes both that it should live in this way as long as it lives, and that when it meets its end it will enter what is akin and of the same kind, and will be separated from human evils. So, given that sort of sustenance, there is no risk of its fearing, Simmias and Cebes,[*38] that it may be torn apart during its separation from the body and blown apart by the winds, and then fly away in all directions and no longer be anything anywhere.'

84c Now when Socrates had said that, a long silence fell, and Socrates himself was absorbed in the argument he had given, or so it seemed from his appearance, and most of us were too. But Cebes and Simmias continued to talk with each other in an undertone. Socrates caught sight of them and asked: 'What is it? Do you think that there is something missing in what was said? Because of course it still contains many grounds for suspicion and counter-attack, at least if one is to go right through it properly. Now if the two of you are considering something else, then I'm talking quite beside the point. But if you are at all puzzled about these

84d things, then don't for a moment hang back from speaking out yourselves and explaining, if you think that it would have been said better in some other way, and also from inviting me to help you, if you think that you'll resolve your puzzles any better with my aid.'

Simmias said: 'Very well, Socrates, I'll tell you the truth. For some time each of us has been puzzled, and so we have been prompting each

---

[37] The soul would be working in the opposite way to Penelope in the *Odyssey*; Penelope chose to unravel what she had woven, whereas the soul would reweave what philosophy had unravelled.

[*38] Omitting ταῦτα δ᾽ ἐπιτηδεύσασα (84b4–5), with J. Burnet *Plato's Phaedo* (Oxford, 1911), as a gloss on ἐκ τῆς τοιαύτης τροφῆς.

other and telling each other to ask a question, for, although we're eager for an answer, we're reluctant to trouble you, in case it may be irksome to you because of your present plight.'

When Socrates heard that he chuckled and said: 'Oh dear, Simmias! It would surely be hard for me to persuade other people that I don't consider my present lot a plight, when I can't persuade even the two of you, but instead you worry that I'm in a rather more discontented state now than in my earlier life. You seem to think that I'm worse at prophecy than the swans: though they sing at earlier times too, it is when they realize they must die that they sing longest and most of all,[39] overjoyed that they are about to depart to meet the god whose servants they are. But because of their own fear of death human beings tell lies about the swans as well, and say that it is out of distress that they leave with a song, lamenting their death; they do not keep in mind the fact that no bird sings when hungry, cold, or in some other kind of distress, not even the nightingale herself, or the swallow or the hoopoe, the very birds said to sing in lament from distress. But these birds do not seem to me to sing because of distress, and nor do the swans, but since, I believe, they belong to Apollo, they are prophetic and know in advance the good things in Hades, and so they sing in delight on that day more than at earlier times. Now I believe that I myself am the swans' fellow-slave and sacred to the same god, and have prophecy from my master no less than they do, and am being separated from my life with no more regret than they are. No, as far as that is concerned, you should say and ask whatever you want, for as long as eleven Athenian men[40] permit.'

'Good,' said Simmias. 'I'll tell you what puzzles me, and Cebes here in his turn will say in what respect he doesn't accept what has been said. Well, I think, Socrates, as perhaps you do too, that knowing the clear truth about things like this in our present life is either impossible or something extremely difficult, but that all the same not testing from every angle what is said about them, refusing to give up until one is exhausted from considering it in every way, is the mark of an extremely feeble sort of man. Because concerning them one ought surely to achieve *one* of the following: either to learn or discover how things are, or, if it is impossible

84e

85a

85b

85c

---

[39] Retaining the MSS reading μάλιστα at 85a1–2, with W.J. Verdenius, 'Notes on Plato's *Phaedo*', *Mnemosyne* 4.11 (1958), 193–243 and Christopher Rowe, *Plato: Phaedo* (Cambridge, 1993). Others emend to κάλλιστα, yielding the translation 'longest and most beautifully'.

[40] See p. 45 n. 7 above.

85d to do that, at least to take the best human proposition – the hardest one to disprove – and to ride on that as if one were taking one's chances on a raft, and to sail through life in that way, unless one could get through the journey with more safety and less precariousness on a more solid vehicle, some divine proposition. Certainly on this occasion I won't be ashamed to ask my question, now that you yourself say as much, and so I won't be able to blame myself later for not having said now what I think. For, Socrates, ever since I've been considering what has been said, both on my own and with Cebes here, it hasn't seemed entirely sufficient.'

85e Socrates said: 'Yes, my friend, and maybe you're right. But tell me in just what respect it seems insufficient.'

'In the following respect, I think,' he said. 'One might say the same thing about attunement too, and a lyre and strings: that the attunement is

86a something invisible, incorporeal, and utterly beautiful and divine in the tuned lyre, whereas the lyre itself and its strings are bodies, corporeal, composite and earthy, and akin to the mortal. So when someone either smashes the lyre or cuts and snaps its strings, what if one were to insist, with the same argument as yours, that the attunement must still exist and not have perished? For there would be no way, when the lyre still exists with its strings snapped, and when the strings themselves, which

86b are of a mortal kind, still exist, that the attunement, which is akin to and of the same nature as the divine and immortal, could have perished, and perished before the mortal did. No, he'd say, the attunement must still exist on its own somewhere, and the bits of wood and the strings must rot away before anything happens to the attunement. In actual fact, Socrates, I think that you yourself are well aware that we[41] take the soul to be something of precisely this kind, since our body is made taut, so to speak, and held together by hot, cold, dry, wet and certain other such things,

86c and our soul is a blend and attunement of those very things, when they are blended properly and proportionately with one another.

'Anyway, if the soul really is a sort of attunement, obviously when our body is loosened or tautened beyond proportion by illnesses or other evils, the soul must perish at once, however divine it may be, just like other sorts of attunement, both those consisting in sounds and those in

---

[41] This seems to refer to an unspecified Pythagorean circle, which includes Echecrates (88d) as well as Simmias, and has strong associations with the recorded views of Philolaus on 'attunements' (Greek *harmoniai*; see C. Huffman, 'Philolaus', in the online *Stanford Encyclopedia of Philosophy*), even though no reliable source explicitly attributes to him the thesis that soul is an attunement.

all the products of the craftsmen, whereas each body's remains must last for a long time, until they are burned up or rot away. So consider what we'll say in reply to this argument, should someone claim that the soul is a blend of the things in the body, and so is the first thing to perish in what is called "death".' 86d

Socrates now looked across with wide eyes, as he often used to do, smiled and said: 'Yes, a fair point from Simmias. So if one of you can resolve the difficulty better than I can, why not answer him? For in fact he seems to be getting to grips with the argument with some success. However, before we answer I think that we should wait to hear from Cebes here what charge he for his part has to bring against the argument, so that in due time we can decide what to say; and then after we've heard from him we should either concede the point to them, if they seem to be hitting a right note, or, if not, then and only then plead in the argument's defence. So come on,' he said, 'Cebes, take your turn and tell us what it was that was troubling you.' 86e

'I'll tell you,' said Cebes. 'Well, the argument seems still to be where it was, and to be open to the same charge that we were making earlier. That our soul existed even before it entered its present form, I don't retreat from saying that this has been very neatly and, if it isn't tasteless to say so, quite sufficiently proved. But that it also still exists somewhere after we have died – there I don't think the point has been proved. Now I don't accept Simmias' objection that soul isn't something tougher and longer-lasting than body, for I think it is far superior indeed in all those respects. "So why are you still doubtful," the argument would say, "when you see that the *weaker* one still exists when the human being has died? Don't you think that the longer-lasting one must still be kept intact during this time?" 87a

'Consider then whether there is anything in my response to that. It seems, you see, that like Simmias I too need a sort of simile. For I think that the way in which these points are made is the same as if one were to give the following argument about a human being, a weaver who had died in old age. One might argue that the human being has not perished but exists intact somewhere, providing as evidence the fact that the cloak that he himself wove for his own use and wore is intact and has not perished. Should someone doubt him, he'd ask which is the longer-lasting kind of thing: a human being or a cloak that is in use and frequently worn. When the other replied that the human being is by far the longer-lasting kind, 87b

87c

he'd suppose that it had been proved that the human being was therefore certainly intact, since the *shorter*-lasting one hadn't perished.

'But in actual fact, Simmias, I think it isn't like that – for you too should consider what I'm saying. Everyone would protest that that is a simple-minded thing for someone to say; for that weaver of mine wore out and wove for himself many such cloaks, and then perished after the whole lot of them; and this was presumably before the last one, yet a human being is not, for all that, inferior to a cloak or weaker than it. Soul in its relation to body would, I think, warrant this same image, and someone who says these same things about them would seem to me to be saying something quite reasonable, that the soul is long-lasting, the body weaker and shorter-lasting. None the less, he'd say, although each soul wears out many bodies, especially if it lives for many years (because if the body is in flux and perishing when the human being is still alive, the soul still always reweaves what is being worn out), all the same, when the soul perishes it must at that moment have its last piece of weaving and perish before that one alone. And, after the soul perishes, only then does the body show its natural weakness and quickly rot and disappear. And so it is not right as yet to put one's trust in this argument and be confident that our soul still exists somewhere after we have died.

'Let us suppose someone conceded even more to one who says what you are saying,[42] and granted him not only that our souls existed during the time before we were even born, but also that, after we have died, there is nothing to prevent the souls of some people from still existing and from being destined to go on existing, to be born many times and to die again, on the grounds that the soul is so tough in nature that it can endure being born many times. But let us suppose that, after granting this much, he refused to concede the further point that the soul does not suffer in its many births and at the end perish completely during one of those deaths, and that he said that no one knows which death and which parting from the body make the soul perish. Because, he would say, none of us can observe that. Now if this is so, nobody who is confident in the face of death can fail to be displaying unintelligent confidence, unless he can prove that soul is altogether immortal and imperishable. Otherwise

87d

87e

88a

88b

---

[42] Deleting ἤ in 88a2. If it is retained we should translate: 'let us suppose one conceded to someone saying even more than what you are saying'.

someone about to die must always fear for his own soul that it may perish completely in its imminent disconnection from the body.'

Now when we all heard them say this our mood took an unpleasant turn, as we later told each other, because we had been firmly persuaded by the earlier argument, but then they seemed to have disturbed us all over again and sent us plummeting into doubt, not just about the arguments given before, but also about what would be said later. We were worried that we might be worthless as judges, or even that the very facts of the matter might merit doubt.

ECHECRATES: Heavens, Phaedo, I quite sympathize with you. Now that I too have heard you, it makes me too say something like this to myself: 'What argument will we still trust now? How utterly persuasive the argument was that Socrates was giving, yet now it has been plunged into doubt!' You see, this theory that our soul is a kind of attunement has an extraordinary hold on me, both at this moment and at all times, and now that it has been mentioned it has reminded me, as it were, that I myself too had already come to believe this. I really need some other argument, a brand-new one, that will persuade me that when someone has died his soul does not die with him. So for heaven's sake tell me how Socrates pursued the argument. Was he too at all noticeably upset, as you say the rest of you were, or did he instead come calmly to the argument's rescue? And was his help sufficient, or inadequate? Please go through everything for us as accurately as you can.

PHAEDO: Well, Echecrates, I'd often admired Socrates, but I never respected him more than when I was with him then. Now perhaps there is nothing surprising in his having something to say. But I particularly admired in him first how pleasantly, genially and respectfully he took in the young men's argument, then how discerningly he noticed the effect the arguments had had on us, and next how well he cured us and rallied us when we'd taken to our heels in defeat, so to speak, and spurred us on to follow at his side and consider the argument with him.

ECHECRATES: So how did he do so?

PHAEDO: I'll tell you. I happened to be sitting to his right, on a stool next to the couch, and he was sitting much higher up than I was. Now he gave my head a stroke and squeezed the hairs on my neck – he had the habit of poking fun at my hair from time to time – and said: 'So tomorrow, Phaedo, I expect you'll cut off these beautiful locks.'

'I suppose so, Socrates,' I said.

88c

88d

88e

89a

89b

'You won't, if you follow my advice.'

'What then?'

89c 'I'll cut off my locks,' he said, 'and you'll cut off these ones today – if our argument dies and we can't revive it. As for me, if I were you and the argument escaped me, I'd swear an oath like the Argives[43] not to grow my hair long until I return to combat and defeat the argument of Simmias and Cebes.'

'But,' I said, 'even Heracles, as the story goes, couldn't fight against two.'

'Well, call for *me*,' he said, 'as your Iolaus,[44] while it's still light.'

'Then I call for you,' I said, 'not as Heracles, but as Iolaus calling Heracles.'

'It won't make any difference,' he said. 'But first let's make sure that a certain thing doesn't happen to us.'

'What sort of thing?' I asked.

89d 'Becoming haters of arguments,' he said, 'like those who come to hate people. Because there's no greater evil that could happen to one than hating arguments. Hating arguments and hating people come about in the same way. For misanthropy sets in as a result of putting all one's trust in someone and doing so without expertise, and taking the person to be entirely truthful, sound and trustworthy, and then a little later finding him to be wicked and untrustworthy – and then again with someone else. When this happens to someone many times, particularly with those

89e whom he would take to be his very closest friends, and he has been falling out with people again and again, he ends up hating everyone and thinking that there is nothing sound in anyone at all. Haven't you ever seen this happen?'

'I certainly have,' I said.

'Now this is deplorable,' he said, 'and obviously someone like that was trying to deal with people without having expertise in human qualities, wasn't he? For surely if he had been doing so with expertise he'd have

90a viewed matters as they really are: he would have recognized that both the very good and the very wicked are few in number, and that those in between are the most numerous.'

'What do you mean?' I asked.

---

43 According to Herodotus (1.82) the Argives swore that they would not grow their hair long until they recovered Thyreae from the Spartans.
44 Heracles' charioteer and assistant.

'It's just like the very small and large,' he said. 'Do you think there is anything rarer than discovering a very large or very small person, or dog, or anything else? Or similarly one that is swift or slow, ugly or beautiful, light or dark? Haven't you observed that in all such cases the far extremities are rare and few, while those in between are plentiful and numerous?'

'Certainly,' I said.

'So do you think,' he said, 'that if a competition in wickedness were   90b
set up, here too very few would come to the fore?'

'That's likely enough,' I said.

'Yes, it is likely,' he said. 'All the same, arguments do not resemble people in that way (I was following your lead just now), but in the following way: when someone without expertise in arguments trusts an argument to be true, and then a little later thinks that it is false, sometimes when it is, sometimes when it isn't, and when he does the same again with one argument after another. This applies particularly to those who   90c
have spent time dealing with the arguments used in disputation. As you know, they end up thinking that they have become very wise, and that they alone have understood that there is nothing sound or firm in any thing or in any argument, but that all things turn back and forth, exactly as if in the Euripus,[45] and do not stay put for any time.'

'That's quite true,' I said.

'Now, Phaedo,' he said, 'it would be a lamentable fate if there really were some true and firm argument that could be understood, and yet   90d
from associating with arguments of another sort – the very same ones seeming true at some times but not at others – someone were to blame not himself or his own lack of expertise, but instead because of his agitation were to end up gratefully transferring the blame from himself to the arguments, and from that point to spend the rest of his life hating and belittling arguments, deprived of both truth and knowledge about things.'

'Yes,' I said, 'that would be lamentable indeed.'

'So first let's make sure we avoid this,' he said, 'and let's not allow into   90e
our soul the notion that there's probably nothing sound in arguments. It will be much better to assume that *we* are not sound yet, but must make a

---

[45] A strait separating Euboea from the Greek mainland, where the current frequently reverses direction.

manly effort to be sound. You and the others should do this for the sake
91a of your whole life to come, but I for the sake of my death considered in
its own right, because concerning that very thing I'm now in danger of
desiring not wisdom but victory, like those who are utterly uneducated.
For when they are at odds about something, they also do not care about
the facts of the matter they are arguing about, but strive to make what
they themselves have proposed seem true to those who are present. And
I think that now I will differ from them only to this extent: I won't
strive to make what I say seem true to those who are present, except as a
byproduct, but instead to make it seem so as much as possible to myself.

91b For I reckon, my dear friend – see how ambitious I'm being – that if what
I'm saying is actually true, then it's quite right to be convinced; if, on
the other hand, there is nothing in store for one who has died, at least in
this period before I die I will be less of a mournful burden to those who
are with me, and this folly won't stay with me – that would have been an
evil – but will perish shortly. This then, Simmias and Cebes, is the
baggage I bring with me when approaching the argument. But as for you,

91c if you take my advice, you'll give little thought to Socrates and much
more to the truth: if you think I say something true, agree with me, and
if not, use every argument to resist me, making sure that my eagerness
doesn't make me deceive myself and you simultaneously, and that I don't
leave my sting in you, like a bee, before I depart.

'Well, come on,' he said. 'First remind me what you were saying, in
case I turn out not to remember. Now Simmias, I believe, has doubts
and fears that even though the soul is something both more divine

91d and more beautiful than the body, it may perish first, because it is a
sort of attunement. Cebes, on the other hand, seemed to me to grant
me this point – that soul is longer-lasting than body – but to suppose
that nobody can be certain whether, after wearing out *many* bodies in
a long sequence, upon leaving behind its last body the soul may not
itself perish, and whether death may not be this very thing, soul's perishing, since body for its part has no rest at all from its constant perishing. Aren't these just the points, Simmias and Cebes, that we must
consider?'

91e They both then agreed that those were the points to consider.
'Well,' he said, 'do you not accept any of the previous arguments, or
do you accept some but not others?'
'Some,' the two of them said, 'but not others.'

'What then,' he asked, 'do you say about that argument in which we said that learning is recollection, and that since this is the case our soul must exist somewhere else before it gets bound in the body?' 92a

'As for me,' said Cebes, 'back then I was incredibly convinced by it, and now I stand by it more than by any other argument.'

'Yes, this is true of me too,' said Simmias, 'and I'd be greatly surprised if I were ever to change my mind, at least about *that*.'

To which Socrates said: 'Well, my Theban visitor, you must change your mind, if the notion remains that attunement is a composite thing, and that soul is composed, as a sort of attunement, of the features of the body when these are held taut. For presumably you won't allow 92b yourself to say that an attunement existed, already composed, before those things existed of which it was due to be composed. Or will you?'

'Not at all, Socrates,' he said.

'Then do you realize,' he said, 'that this is what you do turn out to be saying when you assert that the soul exists even before it enters a human form or body, and that it exists despite being composed of things that do not yet exist? Because an attunement is not like the thing to which you are comparing it: the lyre, its strings and its notes come into being 92c beforehand, still untuned, and the attunement comes together last of all, and is the first to perish. So how will this argument of yours work in concert with that other one?'

'It simply can't,' answered Simmias.

'Yet if there is any argument that should work in concert,' he said, 'it's one about *attunement*!'

'True,' said Simmias.

'This argument of yours, then, doesn't work in concert. Consider which of the two arguments you choose, that learning is recollection, or that soul is attunement?'

'The first one, Socrates,' he said, 'by far. For the second has come 92d to me with no proof but with a sort of plausibility and outward appeal, which is the basis on which most people believe it too. But I am aware that arguments that give their proofs by means of what is plausible make hollow claims, and unless one guards oneself very well against them are utterly deceitful, both in geometry and in all other subjects. The argument about recollection and learning, on the other hand, has been provided by means of a hypothesis worthy of acceptance. Because it was said[46] I think that it is as certain that our soul existed even before it entered a body as that there exists in its own right the being that bears the label "what it is". And I have accepted that hypothesis, or so I convince myself, on both sufficient and correct grounds. So for these reasons, it seems, I mustn't allow myself or anyone else to say that soul is attunement.'

'Now what if you consider it in the following way, Simmias?' he asked. 'Do you think that an attunement or any other kind of compound is the sort of thing to be in some state different from that of its components?'

'Not at all.'

'And not the sort of thing either, I suppose, to do something or have something done to it beyond what those things either do or have done to them?'

He concurred.

'In that case, an attunement is not the sort of thing to *govern* its components, but rather to follow them.'

He thought so too.

'Then there is not a remote chance of an attunement making a movement or a sound opposed to its own parts, or opposing them in some other way.'

'No, not a chance.'

'Next, isn't each attunement naturally an attunement according to the way in which it was tuned?'

'I don't understand,' he said.

'Isn't it the case,' he said, 'that if it were tuned more and to a greater extent – assuming that this can happen – it would be more of an attunement and would be a greater one, whereas if it were tuned less and to an inferior extent, it would be a lesser and inferior one?'

'Yes, absolutely.'

'Now is this true of soul? That is to say, is one soul in even the smallest degree this very thing, soul, more and to a greater extent than another, or less so and to an inferior extent?'

'No, in no way whatever,' he replied.

'Come on then,' he said, 'in heaven's name. Is it said that while one soul has intelligence and virtue and is good, another has unintelligence and wickedness and is bad? And is it truly said?'

92e

93a

93b

93c

---

[46] At 76e–77a.

'Of course it's true.'

'Well, take those people who have proposed that soul is attunement. How will one of them describe these things – virtue and vice – which are in our souls? As a further kind of attunement and non-attunement? And will they say that one soul – the good one – has been tuned and contains another attunement, when it itself is an attunement, but that another soul is itself untuned and does not contain another attunement?'

'I for one can't say,' said Simmias. 'But clearly someone who adopted this hypothesis would say some such thing.'

'But it has already been agreed,' he said, 'that one soul is no more nor less soul than another one, and the agreement comes to the following: one attunement is not an attunement any more or to a greater extent, nor less or to an inferior extent, than another one. Correct?' 93d

'Entirely.'

'Good, and if it is not at all more nor less an attunement, it is neither more nor less tuned. Is that right?'

'It is.'

'And if it is neither more nor less tuned, can it have a greater or lesser share of attunement, or only an equal one?'

'An equal one.'

'Now since one soul is no more nor less this very thing, soul, than another, it isn't more tuned, or less tuned either?' 93e

'Quite so.'

'Right, and if this is true of soul, a soul could not have any greater share of non-attunement, or for that matter of attunement?'

'No, certainly not.'

'And now if *this* is true of soul, could one soul have any greater share of vice or virtue than another, if, that is, vice were non-attunement and virtue attunement?'

'No, no greater at all.'

'Or rather, Simmias, according to the correct argument, presumably no soul will have a share of vice if it is an attunement; for since an attunement is, of course, completely this very thing, an attunement, it could never have a share of non-attunement.' 94a

'Definitely not.'

'Nor of course, since a soul is completely a soul, could it have a share of vice.'

'No, how could it, given what's been said already?'

'In that case, by this argument we find that all souls of all living creatures will be good to the same extent, if it is the nature of souls to be this very thing, souls, to the same extent.'

'I think so, Socrates,' he said.

'Do you find it acceptable,' said Socrates, 'that this should be said, and
94b that such should be the upshot of the argument, if the hypothesis that soul is attunement were correct?'

'No, in no way whatever,' replied Simmias.

'Next,' he said, 'of all the things in a human being, is there any other than soul that you would say is in command, and especially a wise soul?'

'No, I wouldn't.'

'Does soul do so by surrendering to the body's affections or by actually opposing them? What I mean is something like the following. When heat and thirst are there inside, the soul pulls towards the opposite, not drinking, and when hunger is there inside, the soul pulls towards not eating. And there are surely countless other ways
94c in which we see the soul opposing what belongs to the body, aren't there?'

'Certainly.'

'Now, again, didn't we previously agree that, if it really were an attunement, it would never make music opposed to the way in which its components were tautened, loosened, struck or affected in any other respect, but would instead follow them and never direct them?'

'We did, of course,' he said.

'Well then, don't we discover that in reality it does quite the oppo-
94d site, directing all its alleged components, and opposing them almost everywhere through its entire life, and playing the master in every way, correcting some of them – those to which gymnastics and medicine are appropriate – more ruthlessly and with certain hardships, but others more gently, some with threats, others with reprimands, conversing with the desires, rages and fears as if it were one thing and they another? Homer himself has, I think, represented this sort of thing in the *Odyssey*,[47] when he says of Odysseus:

He struck his chest and spoke reproachfully to his heart:
94e   "Endure, my heart. You once endured something even more shameful."

---

[47] At 20.17–18.

'Now do you suppose that when Homer composed this he thought that soul is attunement and the sort of thing to be led by the body's affections? Didn't he think instead that soul is the sort of thing to lead them and play the master, and that it is something far more divine than befits an attunement?'

'I do indeed think so, Socrates.'

'In that case, my excellent friend, it isn't in any way right for us to say that soul is a sort of attunement. If we did, it seems we'd be agreeing   95a
neither with Homer, a divine poet, nor with ourselves.'

'Quite so,' he said.

'Well then,' said Socrates, 'it seems that Theban Harmonia[48] and her kind have become fairly propitious to us. But what about Cadmus and his kind, Cebes? How and with what argument will we propitiate them?'

'You'll discover it, I believe,' said Cebes. 'Certainly this argument which you gave in answer to attunement was astonishingly contrary to my expectations. You see, when Simmias spoke up because he was puzzled, I really did wonder whether anyone would have any way of dealing with   95b
his argument. It thus seemed to me quite extraordinary that it didn't withstand the very first attack of your own argument. So I wouldn't be surprised if the same things happened to Cadmus' argument too.'

'Don't go making bold claims, my friend,' said Socrates, 'in case some malign power turns our upcoming argument to flight. Anyway, god will see to that, but let us in Homeric style come to close quarters and test whether there actually is something in what you're saying. Now then, the gist of what you're seeking is as follows. You think it must be demon-
strated that our soul is both imperishable and immortal, if it is not to be   95c
unintelligent and foolish for a philosophical man to believe confidently, when he is about to die, that after his death he will fare better there than if he had lived a different life before he met his end. As for showing that the soul is something tough and godlike, and that it existed even before we became human beings – there is nothing, you say, to stop all of that being evidence not of immortality, but of the fact that soul is long-lasting and existed somewhere previously for an unimaginably long time, and used to know and do a great deal. Anyhow, you said, that does not make   95d
it any the more immortal: on the contrary, the very fact of coming into

---

[48] The wife of Cadmus, legendary founder of Thebes. Socrates refers to Simmias' objection (*harmonia* being the Greek word translated 'attunement').

a human body was the start of its perishing, like a disease. On this view, the soul really suffers as it lives this life and eventually, in what is called "death", it perishes. Now whether it enters a body once or many times makes no difference, you claim, at least as regards the fear each of us has. For anyone of any intelligence *should* be afraid, if they do not know that

95e   it is immortal and cannot offer an argument to show as much. This is the sort of thing, Cebes, that I think you're saying. I'm deliberately going back over it repetitively to make sure nothing escapes us, and to let you add or take away something if you want.'

To which Cebes said: 'No, I don't want to take away or add anything now. That's just what I'm saying.'

Now Socrates paused for quite some time and considered something by himself, and then said: 'What you're seeking is no small matter, Cebes; we must study thoroughly and as a whole the cause of coming-to-be and

96a   ceasing-to-be. So, if you like, I'll recount my experiences concerning them; then, if you see something useful in what I say, you'll use it to convince yourself about the very points you raise.'

'But of course I'd like that,' said Cebes.

'Then listen, because I'm going to tell you. Well, Cebes,' he said, 'when I was young I became incredibly eager for the sort of wisdom that they call research into nature. That used to strike me as quite sublime: to know the causes of each thing, why each one comes to be, why it perishes, and why

96b   it is. Time and again I would shift in different directions, considering first the following sort of questions. Is it when the hot and the cold start to decompose, as some people were saying, that living things grow into a unity? Is it because of blood that we think, or air, or fire? Or is it none of these, but is it rather the brain that supplies the senses of hearing, seeing and smelling, and do memory and opinion come to be from them, and when memory and opinion become stable, does knowledge come to be from them along these same lines? Next I considered the way in

96c   which these things cease to be, and the events that affect the heaven and the earth. And in the end I myself came to think that I was uniquely unqualified for this inquiry.

'I'll give you ample evidence for this: I was so utterly blinded by that inquiry with regard to the very things that, at least as I and others supposed, I had previously known clearly that I unlearned those very things that earlier I had thought I knew, on many subjects, but in particular why a human being grows. Because earlier I thought it obvious to everyone

that it is on account of eating and drinking. For whenever portions of 96d
flesh have been added from food to other portions of flesh, and portions
of bone to portions of bone, and so too by the same principle stuff of their
own kind has been added to each of the other stuffs, it is then, I thought,
that that which was a small mass has gone on to become a big one; and
that is how the small person comes to be large. That's what I supposed
then. Reasonably enough, don't you think?'

'Yes, I do,' said Cebes.

'Then consider the following as well. I thought my belief satisfactory
when a large person standing by a small one seemed to be larger because 96e
of the head itself, and so likewise when one horse was compared with
another. Yes, and it seemed to me even more obvious that ten was more
numerous than eight on account of there being two added to it, and that
two cubits was larger than one on account of its exceeding the other
because of a half.'

'But now what do you think about them?' asked Cebes.

'That I'm no doubt a long way indeed from thinking that I know
the cause of any of these. I don't allow myself to say even that, when
somebody adds one to one, either the one it was added to has become
two,[49] or the one that was added and the one it was added to became 97a
two, on account of the addition of the first to the second. For I find it
astonishing that when each of them was apart from the other, each turned
out to be one, and they weren't two at that time, but when they came
near each other, this supposedly became a cause of their coming to be
two, namely the union that consisted in being put near each other. No,
nor can I still persuade myself that if somebody divides one, this, the
division, has now become a cause of its coming to be two. For then there
comes to be a cause of coming to be two that is the opposite of the earlier
cause. Back then, you see, it was because they were brought together into 97b
proximity with each other, and one was added to the other, but now it
is because they are brought apart, and one is separated from the other.
No, and I can no longer persuade myself that by using this approach I
know why one comes to be, nor, in short, why anything else comes to be,
or perishes, or is. Instead I throw together on impulse my own different
kind of approach, and I don't adopt this one at all.

---

[49] Omitting the words (ἢ τὸ προστεθέν) suggested at 96e9 by D. Wyttenbach, *Platonis Phaedon*
(Leiden 1810 and Leipzig 1825). These words raise a further possibility: 'the one that was added'
has become two.

'However, one day I heard somebody reading from what he said was a
97c book by Anaxagoras, and saying that it turns out to be intelligence that
both orders things and is cause of everything. I was pleased with this
cause, and it struck me that in a way it is good that intelligence should
be cause of everything, and I supposed that, if this is the case, when
intelligence is doing the ordering it orders everything and assigns each
thing in whatever way is best. So, I thought, should someone want to
discover the cause of how each thing comes to be, perishes, or is, this is
97d what he must find out about it: how it is best for it either to be, or to act
or be acted upon in any other respect whatsoever. What is more, on this
theory a human being should consider nothing other than what is optimal
or best, concerning both that thing itself and everything else. The same
person is bound to know the worse too, for it is the same knowledge that
concerns them both. So by reasoning like this I thought to my delight
that I had found in Anaxagoras a teacher of the cause of things who fitted
my own intelligence. I supposed that he would tell me first whether the
97e earth was flat or round, and, when he had done so, would also explain
the cause that necessitated it, saying what was better – better, that is, that
the earth should be like this. And if he said that it was in the centre,
98a he would also explain, I thought, that it was better that it should be in
the centre. If he showed me these things, I was ready to stop wishing
for any other kind of cause. In particular, I was equally ready to learn
about the sun in that way, and about the moon and the other celestial
bodies, about their relative speed and turnings and the other things they
underwent, namely how it is better that each of them should both act and
be acted upon as it is. For given his claim that they have been ordered
by intelligence, I never thought that he would introduce a cause for them
98b other than its being best that they should be as they are. So I supposed
that when he assigned the cause to each of them and in common to them
all, he would also explain what was best for each, and the good common
to them all. And I wouldn't have signed away my hopes for a large sum,
but I got hold of his books with real excitement and started reading them
as quickly as I could, so that I might know as quickly as possible what was
best and what was worse.

'But then, my friend, I was swept away from my marvellous expectations, for as I went on reading it I saw the man making no use of his
98c intelligence and not laying any causes at its door with regard to ordering
things, but assigning the causality to air, aether, water and the like, as

well as many other oddities. And I came to think that what had happened to him was exactly as if someone said that it is because of intelligence that Socrates does everything that he does, but then, when he undertook to give the causes of each of my actions, were to say, first, that the cause of my now sitting here is because my body is composed of bones and sinews, and whereas the bones are rigid and have joints separating them from each other, the sinews can tauten and relax, and they sur- 98d round the bones, together with the bits of flesh and the skin that keeps them together. Now while the bones are supported in their sockets, the sinews loosen and tauten and so, presumably, enable me to bend my limbs now, and on account of that cause I'm bent here in the sitting position. Next he'd give other such causes with regard to my conversing with you, assigning the causality to voices, airs and ears, and to countless other such things, and would have neglected to give the real 98e causes, namely that, since the Athenians have decided that it was better to condemn me, on account of that I too have also decided that it is better to sit here, and more just to stay put and suffer whatever punishment they decree. For by the Dog, I think these sinews and bones 99a would long have been in Megara or Boeotia, transported by an opinion as to what is best, if I didn't think it more just and honourable to suffer whatever punishment the city imposes, rather than to escape and run away.

'Now calling such things *causes* is extremely odd. But if someone said that without having such things – bones, sinews and whatever else I have – I wouldn't be able to do what I have decided, he'd be telling the truth. However, saying that it is on account of them that I do what I do, rather than because of my choice of what is best, despite the fact that I 99b act because of intelligence – that would be a profoundly careless way to talk. Imagine not being able to make the distinction that the real cause is one thing, while that without which the cause could never be a cause is something else! That is just what most people seem to me to call a cause, fumbling in the dark, as it were, and using a name that belongs to something else. That is why one individual puts a vortex around the earth and thus makes the earth actually be kept stationary by the heaven, while another compares it to a flat kneading-trough and props it up with air. But as for these things' ability to be positioned now in the best possible 99c way for them to be placed, they neither seek it nor suppose that it has any divine might; instead they believe that one day they might find an

Atlas[50] that is mightier and more immortal and keeps everything together more than this one does, and they do not suppose for a moment that what is good and binding truly does bind and keep anything together.

'Now I would gladly become anyone's pupil to learn just what the truth is about that sort of cause. But since I was denied it and haven't been able 99d either to find it myself or to learn it from someone else, would you like me to give you a demonstration, Cebes, of how I've pursued my second voyage in search of the cause?'

'I'd like that enormously,' he said.

'Well then,' said Socrates, 'I decided after that, when I'd given up looking into things, that I must make sure I didn't suffer the fate of those who view and study the sun in an eclipse. For some of them ruin their 99e eyes, I believe, if they don't study its image in water or something of the kind. I too had that sort of thought, and I started to worry that I might be utterly blinded in my soul through observing things with my eyes and seeking to get hold of them with each of my senses. So I decided that I should take refuge in theories and arguments[51] and look into the truth 100a of things in them. Now maybe in a way it does not resemble what I'm comparing it to. For I don't at all accept that someone who, when studying things, does so in theories and arguments, is looking into them in images any more than someone who does so in facts. In any case, that is how I started out: on every occasion I hypothesize whatever theory I deem most robust, and then I set down as true whatever I think harmonizes with it – both about cause and about everything else – and as false whatever doesn't. I want, though, to tell you more clearly what I'm talking about. I think that at the moment you don't understand.'

'Indeed I don't' said Cebes, 'not altogether.'

100b 'This is what I'm talking about,' he said, 'nothing new, but what I've never stopped talking about, on any other occasion or in particular in the argument thus far. Well, I'll set about giving you a demonstration of the sort of cause which I've pursued. I'll go back to those things that have been our frequent refrain, and start from them, first hypothesizing that there are such things as a Beautiful alone by itself, and a Good, a Large and all the rest. If you grant me these and accept that they exist, I

---

[50] The fallen Titan Atlas, in Greek myth condemned to holding the heaven aloft, here symbolizes the force that keeps both earth and heaven in their places.

[51] Here and in 100a 'theories and arguments' translates one Greek word (*logoi*) which can have either meaning. The singular (*logos*) is translated 'theory' in 100a.

hope to use them to demonstrate to you the cause,[52] and to discover that the soul is immortal.'

'Yes, I do grant you that,' said Cebes, 'so proceed as quickly as you can.'

'Then consider,' he said, 'if the next point seems to you as it does to me. It appears to me that if anything is beautiful other than the Beautiful itself, it is beautiful on account of nothing other than its having a share of *that* Beautiful. And that is what I say about them all. Do you accept that sort of cause?'

'I do,' he said.

'Well then,' he said, 'I no longer understand those other wise causes, and I can't recognise them either. Suppose someone tells me why something or other is beautiful, and says that it is because it has a vivid colour or shape, or some other such thing. I ignore those other explanations, because I am confused when they are all around me, and I keep the following at my side, in my straightforward, amateurish and perhaps simple-minded way: nothing makes it beautiful other than that Beautiful's presence, or association, or whatever its mode and means of accruing may be.*[53] For I don't go so far as to insist on this, but only that it is because of the beautiful that all beautiful things are beautiful. For I think that it is safest to give this reply both to myself and to another, and I believe that if I cling to this I could never fall, but that it is safe to reply both to myself and to anyone else that it is because of the beautiful that beautiful things come to be beautiful. Don't you think so too?'

'I do.'

'In that case, is it also because of largeness that large things come to be large and larger things larger, and because of smallness that smaller things come to be smaller?'

'Yes.'

'So you too wouldn't agree if someone said that one person was larger than another because of his head,[54] and the smaller one smaller because of the same thing. Instead you'd fervently declare that you yourself say simply that everything larger than something else is larger because of nothing other than largeness, and that it is on account of largeness that

100c

100d

100e

101a

---

[52] That is, the cause of such phenomena as those mentioned in 96b–97b.

*[53] Reading προσγενομένου (100d6) with C. Rowe, *Plato: Phaedo* (Cambridge, 1993).

[54] The causal expression translated 'because of a head' also means 'by a head', expressing the margin of difference.

the thing is larger, whereas what is smaller is smaller because of nothing other than smallness, and it is on account of smallness that the thing is smaller. For I suppose that, if you say that it is because of the head that someone is larger and someone smaller, you would be afraid of being met with a counter-argument: first that it is because of the same thing that the larger is larger and the smaller smaller, and secondly that, even though the head is small, the larger person is larger because of it, and that this

101b would be bizarre, somebody's being large because of something small. Or wouldn't you have those fears?'

Cebes laughed at that, and said: 'Yes, I would.'

'So,' he said, 'would you be afraid to say that ten is more numerous than eight because of two, and that it exceeds eight on account of this cause, rather than because of and on account of numerousness? And that two cubits is larger than one cubit because of a half, rather than because of largeness? For surely there would be the same fear.'

'Certainly,' he said.

101c 'Next, if one were added to one, wouldn't you make sure not to say that the addition was the cause of coming to be two, or that the division was the cause if it were divided? You'd loudly exclaim that you don't know any other way of each thing coming to be except by getting a share of the distinctive being of each thing in which it gets a share; that in these cases you have no cause of coming to be two other than getting a share of twoness; that those things that are going to be two must have a share of this; and that whatever is going to be one must have a share of oneness. But as for those divisions and additions and the other such ingenuities, you'd ignore them and leave them for those wiser than yourself to answer

101d with. But you for your part would, as the saying goes, be scared of your own shadow and inexperience, and you'd cling to that safe part of the hypothesis, and answer accordingly.

'But if someone were to cling to the hypothesis itself, you would ignore him and not answer until you had managed to consider its consequences and see whether or not you found them harmonizing with each other. When, however, you had to give an account of that hypothesis itself, you would do so in the same way, first giving again as another hypothesis whichever higher one seemed best, until you came to something sufficient.

101e But you wouldn't throw together what you were saying all at once, would you, like those who practise disputation, by holding a conversation about both the starting-point and its consequences, at least if you wanted to discover something real? For those other people undoubtedly give that not a single word, and not a single thought either, because, thanks to their wisdom, they are able to mix everything together and still be pleased with themselves. But as for you, if you're one of those who love wisdom, you would, I think, do as I am saying.'

102a

'That's very true,' said Simmias and Cebes together.

ECHECRATES: Indeed, Phaedo, and reasonably so. For I think he put that wonderfully lucidly, even for someone with little intelligence.

PHAEDO: Quite so, Echecrates, and everyone there thought so.

ECHECRATES: Yes, and so do we, who weren't there but are hearing it now. Anyway, what was said after that?

PHAEDO: When these points of his were accepted and it was agreed that each of the Forms exists and that other things receive a share of and are named after the Forms themselves, I think that he next asked: 'So if that's what you are saying, whenever you say that Simmias is larger than Socrates, but smaller than Phaedo, don't you mean that at that time both of these, both largeness and smallness, are in Simmias?'

102b

'Yes, I do.'

'However,' he said, 'do you agree that the truth about "Simmias exceeds Socrates" is not as expressed in these words? For presumably it isn't in Simmias' nature to exceed because of being Simmias, but rather because of the largeness that he happens to have. And do you agree that, again, he does not exceed Socrates because Socrates is Socrates, but because Socrates has smallness relative to his largeness?'

102c

'True.'

'Right, and again that he is not exceeded by Phaedo because Phaedo is Phaedo, but because Phaedo has largeness relative to Simmias' smallness?'

'That's so.'

'In that case, this is how Simmias is labelled both small and large, by being in between the pair of them, offering his smallness to Phaedo's largeness to be exceeded, but providing to Socrates his largeness, which exceeds Socrates' smallness.' He smiled as he said this, and then added: 'I seem to be on the point of talking just like a textbook, but anyway the reality is presumably as I say.'

102d

Cebes agreed.

'Now the reason why I say this is that I want you to come to think as I do. For it seems to me not only that Largeness itself is never willing to be large and small at the same time, but also that the largeness in us never

admits the small, and is not willing to be exceeded, but must do one of two
things, either flee and retreat when its opposite, the small, is approaching
it, or perish when that opposite has approached. It is not willing to stand
its ground by admitting smallness and so be different from what it was.
I myself, for example, do admit and withstand smallness and, while still
being this same man who I am, am small; but that thing is large and does
not have the nerve to be small. In the same way, the small in us is never
willing to come to be, or be, large, nor can any other opposite still be what
it was and at the same time come to be, and be, its opposite, but it either
departs or perishes when this happens to it.'

'That's exactly how it seems to me,' said Cebes.

When one of those present heard this (I don't clearly remember who it
was), he said: 'Heavens, in your earlier arguments didn't you accept the
very opposite of what is now being said, that the larger comes to be from
the smaller, and the smaller from the larger, and that the coming-to-be
of opposites is simply this – from their opposites? But now I think it is
being said that this could never happen.'

Socrates inclined his head and listened, and then said: 'Manfully
recalled, but you're not noticing the difference between what is being
said now and what was said then. Back then, you see, it was said that
opposite thing comes to be from opposite thing, whereas now it is being
said that the opposite by itself could never come to be its own opposite,
neither the opposite in us nor the opposite in nature. Because then, my
friend, we were talking about the things that have the opposites, nam-
ing them after those opposites, whereas now we're talking about those
opposites themselves, from whose presence inside them the things that
are named get their labels. We are saying that the opposites themselves
would never be willing to admit coming to be one another.' As he said
this he looked towards Cebes and said: 'Cebes, surely you too weren't
disturbed by any of what he said?'

'No,' said Cebes, 'I'm not back in that state. All the same, I don't for a
moment say that there aren't many things that do disturb me.'

'In that case,' he said, 'between us we've agreed straightforwardly that
the opposite will never be its own opposite.'

'Quite right,' said Cebes.

'I'd like you to go on to consider the following too,' he said, 'and see
if it turns out that you agree with me. Do you call something "hot", and
something "cold"?'

The margin reference markers: 102e, 103a, 103b, 103c.

'Yes, I do.'

'Are they just what you call "snow" and "fire"?'

'Certainly not.' 103d

'Rather, you call the hot something different from fire, and the cold something different from snow?'

'Yes.'

'But you do believe this much, I think, that while it is snow it will never admit the hot, in the way that we were discussing earlier, and continue to be just what it was, snow, as well as something hot, but when the hot is approaching it will either retreat from the hot or perish.'

'Certainly.'

'Yes, and again when the cold is approaching fire, the fire will either withdraw or perish, but it will never have the nerve to admit the coldness and continue to be just what it was, fire, as well as cold.'

'That's true,' he said. 103e

'So is it true,' he said, 'concerning some things of this sort, that not only does the Form itself merit its own name for all time, but there is also something else that merits it, which is not the same as the Form, but which, whenever it exists, always has the feature of that Form. Maybe what I mean will be clearer still in the following case: presumably the odd must always be given this name that we are now uttering, mustn't it?'

'Certainly.'

'Is it the only thing of which that is true – this is my question – or is there also something else, which is not just what the odd is, but all 104a the same must always be called "odd" too, together with its own name, because its nature is such that it is never deprived of the odd? By this I mean, for example, the state in which threeness is, and many other things too. Consider the case of threeness. Don't you think that threeness should always be called both by its own name and by the name of the odd? The odd is not just what threeness is, but nevertheless threeness, fiveness, and an entire half of the number series are somehow naturally such that 104b each of them is always odd, despite not being just what the odd is. Again, the two, the four and in its turn the entire other column of the number series are each always even, despite not being just what the even is. Do you accept that or not?'

'Of course I do,' he said.

'Well then,' he said, 'take a look at the point I want to make clear. It's the following: not only do those opposites evidently not admit one another, but there are also all those things that are not opposites of one another, but always possess the opposites, and they too seem not to admit whatever form is opposed to the form inside them; instead, when it attacks, evidently they either perish or retreat. Or won't we say that the three will either perish or let anything else happen to it, before it puts up with coming to be even, while still being three?'

'Quite so,' said Cebes.

'And of course twoness isn't the *opposite* of threeness,' he said.

'No, certainly not.'

'In that case, not only do the opposite forms not withstand the attack of one another, but there are also some other things that do not withstand the attack of the opposites.'

'That's very true,' he said.

'So' he said, 'do you want us, if we can, to determine what sort of thing they are?'

'Certainly.'

104d 'Now, Cebes,' he said, 'would they be the following: those that, whatever they occupy, compel it not only to have their own form in each case, but also, invariably, the form of some *opposite* of something as well?'[55]

'What do you mean?'

'Just what we were saying a moment ago. For presumably you know that whatever the form of the three occupies, must not only be three but also be odd.'

'Certainly.'

'So, we're saying, the form that is the opposite of whatever feature makes it so would never impose itself upon something like that.'

'No, it wouldn't.'

'Right, and we found that the form of odd makes it so?'

'Yes.'

'And is the form of the even its opposite?'

'Yes.'

104e 'In that case, the form of the even will never impose itself upon three.'

'No, certainly not.'

'So three has no share of the even.'

<hr>

[55] The construal of this sentence is much debated. That the sense should be more or less as indicated in the translation is confirmed by the paraphrase at 104d; whether the printed Greek text can, without emendation, bear that meaning is less than certain.

'No, no share.'

'In that case, threeness is un-even.'

'Yes.'

'So as regards what I was saying we should determine, namely the sort of things that are not the opposites of something but still do not admit that opposite – such as our present example, threeness, which is not the opposite of the even but all the same does not admit the even, because it always imports the opposite of the even, as twoness imports the opposite of the odd and the fire that of the cold, and as a great many   105a
other things do – anyway, see if you make the determination as follows. Not only does the opposite not admit its opposite, but there is also the thing that imports some opposite to whatever it itself attacks, and this further thing, the one that imports it, never admits the opposite of what is imported. But recollect it once again, for there's no harm in hearing it many times. Five will never admit the form of the even, nor will ten, its double, admit the form of the odd. Now the double is also the opposite of something *else*, but it still will not admit the form of the odd. Nor then   105b
will one-and-a-half, nor the others like it either – the half, and next the third and all the others of the kind – admit the form of the whole, if, that is, you follow and agree that it is so.'

'Yes, I entirely agree, and entirely follow,' he said.

'Then tell me again from the start,' he said. 'And don't give as your answer whatever I say in my question, but follow my example. I say this because, besides that safe answer I gave at first, I see another kind of safety, thanks to what we are saying now. For if you were to ask me what it is that, when it comes to be present in anything's body, makes the thing hot, I will not give that safe, ignorant answer – namely that it is hotness –   105c
but, thanks to what we now say, a more ingenious one: that it is fire. And if you ask what it is that, when it comes to be present in any body, makes the body ill, I will not say that it is illness, but that it is fever. And if asked what it is that, when it comes to be present in any number, makes the number odd, I will not say that it is oddness, but that it is oneness, and so on for the rest. Well, see if you now understand well enough what I want.'

'Yes, quite well enough,' said Cebes.

'So answer,' said Socrates. 'What is it that, when it comes to be present in any body, makes the body alive?'

'It is soul,' he said.

105d 'Now is this always the case?'

'Yes, of course,' he said.

'In that case, whenever soul occupies anything, does soul always come to it bringing life?'

'Yes, it does.'

'Does life have an opposite or not?'

'It does,' he said.

'What?'

'Death.'

'So will soul *never* admit the opposite of what it itself always imports, as has been agreed from what was said earlier?'

'Very much so,' said Cebes.

'Very well. What were we just now calling that which does not admit the form of the even?'

'Un-even,' he said.

'What about that which does not admit the just, and whatever does not admit musical?'

105e 'Un-musical,' he said, 'and the former un-just.'

'Very well. What do we call anything that does not admit death?'

'Immortal,'[56] he said.

'Now soul does not admit death, does it?'

'No.'

'In that case, soul is immortal.'

'Yes, immortal.'

'Very well,' he said. 'Should we say that this has been proved? What do you think?'

'Yes, and most sufficiently, Socrates.'

'Well then, Cebes,' he said. 'If the un-even were necessarily

106a imperishable, three would surely be imperishable, wouldn't it?'

'Yes, of course.'

'Now if the un-hot too were necessarily imperishable, then when some-one brought hot to snow, would the snow withdraw intact and unmelted? For it wouldn't *perish*, at least, nor again would it stand its ground and admit the hotness.'

'That's true,' he said.

---

[56] Greek *athanatos*, 'im-mortal' or 'deathless', is morphologically like the modal formation Socrates has more or less invented immediately above, where 'un-F' means 'incapable of being F'. In the case of 'immortal' the word did indeed already carry that modal sense.

'So too in the same way, I suppose, if the un-cold were imperishable, then when something cold came to fire, the fire would never be extinguished, nor would it perish, but it would depart intact and be gone.'

'Necessarily.'

'Now is it necessary to talk in the following way about the immortal as well? If the immortal is imperishable too, then it is impossible for soul to perish whenever death comes to it. Because, given what was said before, it won't admit death or be dead, just as three won't be even, as we were saying, nor again will the odd, and fire won't be cold, nor will the hotness in the fire. "But," someone might say, "why shouldn't it be that, although the odd does not become even when the even comes to it, as was agreed, the odd perishes, and the even comes to be in place of it?" Now against someone who said this, we'd have no way of defending the claim that it does not perish, since the uneven is not imperishable. For if we'd secured agreement to that, it would be easy for us to defend the claim that when the even comes to them the odd and three depart and are gone. And that is how we'd defend claims about fire, hot and the rest, isn't it?'

'Certainly.'

'So too in the present case, that of the immortal, if we secure agreement that it is imperishable too, then soul would be imperishable as well as being immortal. Otherwise we'd need some other argument.'

'But there's no need,' he said, 'at least on that account. For there would hardly be anything else that does not admit destruction, if the immortal, despite being everlasting, will admit destruction.'

'Yes,' said Socrates, 'and as for god, I suppose, and the Form of Life itself, and any other immortal thing there may be, it would be agreed by everyone that they never perish.'

'Indeed,' he said, 'by all people, certainly, and even more so, I imagine, by gods.'

'So because the immortal is also indestructible, surely soul, if it really is immortal, would also be imperishable, wouldn't it?'

'It absolutely must.'

'In that case, when death attacks the human being, the mortal part of him dies, it seems, whereas the immortal part departs intact and undestroyed, and is gone, having retreated from death.'

'So it appears.'

106b

106c

106d

106e

107a 'And so,' he said, 'more surely than anything, Cebes, soul is immortal and imperishable, and our souls really will exist in Hades.'

'For my part, Socrates,' he said, 'I've nothing else to say against this, nor can I doubt the arguments in any way. If, however, Simmias here or someone else has anything to say, it's as well not to keep silent. For if someone wants to say or hear anything on the subject, I don't know of any other occasion than the present one to which he could defer it.'

107b 'Well,' said Simmias, 'on the strength of what has been said I too no longer have any room for doubt. All the same, because of the magnitude of the issues discussed in our arguments, and because of my low regard for human weakness, I'm compelled still to keep some doubt in my mind about what has been said.'

'Yes, not only that, Simmias,' said Socrates, 'but you're right to say so, and, besides, even if you all[57] find the first hypotheses trustworthy, nonetheless you should consider them more clearly. And if you analyze them well enough, you'll follow the argument, I imagine, as far as a human being can follow it up. Should this itself become clear, then you won't seek anything further.'

'That's true,' he said.

107c 'But, gentlemen,' he said, 'it is right to think *this* much: that if the soul actually is immortal, then it needs to be cared for, not only for the sake of the time in which what we call "living" goes on, but for the sake of all time; and that now the dangers of neglecting the soul really would seem to be dreadful. For if death were separation from everything, it would be a godsend for wicked people to die, and thus be separated both from the body and at the same time, by also losing their soul, from their own vice. As it is, however, since the soul is evidently immortal, it could have no 107d means of safety or of escaping evils, other than becoming both as good and as wise as possible. For the soul comes to Hades with nothing other than its education and its way of life, which are said to confer the very greatest benefit or harm upon one who has died, as soon as his journey there starts. And what is said goes as follows.

'When each person has met his end, his guardian spirit, to whom he was allotted when alive, undertakes to bring him to a certain place, where the 107e assembled individuals must present themselves in court, and then travel

---

[57] Here and in the rest of the paragraph Socrates addresses not only Simmias but also the others present, using the second person plural; the translation 'you all' is used to reflect this.

to Hades with that guide who has been appointed to take them on their journey there. Once there, they are given what they should be given, and stay for however long is needed, and then another guide escorts them back here again, after many long cycles of time. So it turns out that the journey is not as Aeschylus' Telephus says. He says that a straightforward "path" 108a leads to Hades, whereas it seems to me to be neither straightforward nor single. For then there would have been no need for guides, because surely nobody would have gone astray in any direction if the road were a single one. In fact, however, it looks as if the path has many divisions and forks – I say so on the evidence of the sacrifices and customs in our world.

'Now the composed and wise soul follows its guide and is not unaware of what is going on around it. But the soul that is desirous of the body, as I said before,[58] is in a flutter for a long time about the body and about 108b the visible region, resists much and suffers much, and is led away by the appointed spirit only by force and with difficulty. On arrival at the place where the other souls are, a soul that is impure and has performed an impure act, by engaging in unjust killings or perpetrating other deeds which are akin to these and characteristic of kindred souls, is shunned by everyone else: everyone turns away from it, and is unwilling to become either its companion or its guide. The soul wanders alone, in the grip of every deprivation, until certain lengths of time have elapsed, and, when 108c they have gone by, it is by necessity borne into the dwelling suitable for it. On the other hand, each soul that has passed through its life both purely and decently receives gods as companions and as guides alike, and then dwells in the region appropriate to it. Now there are many wondrous regions of the earth, and the earth itself is neither of the nature nor of the size it is believed to be by those who usually talk about it, as I have been convinced by someone.'

To which Simmias said: 'What do you mean by this, Socrates? I too, 108d you see, have heard a good deal about the earth, but not the things that convince you. So I'd enjoy hearing about them.'

'Yes, well, Simmias, I don't think that describing what they are, at any rate, requires the skill of Glaucus.[59] But showing that they are *true* seems

---

[58] At 81b–d.

[59] This may be (a) the Glaucus who contrived an ingenious musical instrument out of four discs, which when struck in unison produced a harmony; (b) Glaucus of Chios, the inventor of welding (Herodotus 1.25); or (c) the Glaucus who possessed some marvellous art, perhaps prophecy, but was lost at sea and became a sea-god, encrusted with barnacles (cf. *Republic* 611c–d). See further, Diskin Clay, 'The art of Glaukos', *American Journal of Philology* 106 (1985), 230–6.

to me to be too difficult for Glaucus' skill. For one thing, I might not even be able to do so myself, and, for another, even if I did have the knowledge, I think that the life left to me, Simmias, isn't enough for the length of the discussion. All the same, there's nothing to stop me from saying what sort
108e of form I've been convinced the earth has, and describing its regions.'

'Well,' said Simmias, 'even that is enough.'

'Very well,' he said. 'I've been convinced, first, that, if the earth is
109a round and in the middle of the heaven, it has no need of air or of any other such necessity to stop it falling, but the uniformity of the heaven on every side and the equilibrium of the earth itself are enough to hold it in place. The reason is that, if a thing in equilibrium is put in the middle of something uniform, it will not be able to lean more or less in any direction, but in its uniform state it will stay in place without leaning. Well then,' he said, 'that is the first thing of which I have been convinced.'

'And rightly so,' said Simmias.

'The next thing, then,' he said, 'is that the earth is extremely large, and
109b that we who live from the Phasis up to the pillars of Heracles dwell in a small part of it, dwelling around the sea like ants or frogs around a pond, while many other people dwell elsewhere in many regions of the same kind. For all over the earth there are many hollows of every different shape and size, into which water, mist and air have flowed together. The earth itself, however, is pure and is set in the pure heaven in which the celestial
109c bodies are, the very heaven which most of those who concern themselves with such things*60 call "aether". Water, mist and air are sediments of aether, and they are always flowing together into the hollows of the earth.

'Now we are unaware that we dwell in the earth's hollows, and we suppose that we dwell up on the earth's surface, just as if someone who dwelt in the middle of the seabed were to suppose that he dwelt on the sea's surface, and, when he saw the sun and the other celestial bodies through the water, were to believe that the sea was the heaven, and because of
109d his slowness and weakness had never yet reached the top of the sea, and had not emerged and raised his head out of the sea into the region here, and then seen how much purer and more beautiful it really is than the region where his kind are, and had not been told by anyone else who had seen it. That is just the condition we too are in; for we dwell in a certain

---

*60 Deleting εἰωθότων λέγειν (109c2), which, as Burnet, *Plato's Phaedo*, argues, seems to have been inserted from 108c7.

hollow of the earth and suppose that we dwell upon its surface, and we call the air "heaven", as if it were the heaven and the celestial bodies moved through it. But in actual fact the same thing happens: because of our weakness and slowness we cannot go all the way to the edge of the air. For if someone were to come to the top of the air, or get wings and fly up there, he would stick his head through and behold the sight: just as in this region fish see the things here if they stick their heads up out of the sea, someone would likewise behold the sight of the things there, and if his nature were good enough to endure viewing them, he would perceive that *that* is the true heaven, the genuine light and the veritable earth. For this earth of ours, its stones and the whole region here are damaged and eaten away, as the things in the sea have been by the brine. Nothing worth mentioning grows in the sea, and there is virtually nothing flawless there, but wherever there actually is earth, there are broken rocks, sand, and an unimaginable amount of filth and mud, and things that are not at all worth comparing with the beauties around us. But those other beauties, in turn, would appear to excel the ones around us much more still. For if it's also appropriate to tell a myth, it's worth hearing, Simmias, what the things on the surface of the earth under the heaven are really like.'

'Well, Socrates' said Simmias, 'we would enjoy hearing this myth.'

'Very well, my friend,' he said. 'It is said first that the earth itself, if one could view it from above, would appear to the eye like one of those balls of twelve leather pieces: varied, and interspersed with colours, of which the colours here are like samples, the ones that painters use. There, however, the entire earth is of such colours, and of colours much brighter and purer still than these. For part of the earth is purple and astonishingly beautiful, part of it is golden, all its white part is whiter than chalk or snow, and the earth is composed of the other colours in the same way, and of colours more numerous and beautiful still than all those which we ourselves have seen. For these hollows of the earth are completely full of water and air, and thus themselves display a pattern of colour as they gleam amid the intricate variety of other colours. The result is that the impression given of the earth is of a single continuous intricate pattern. Given that the earth is like that, the things that grow on it do so in matching style – trees and flowers and their fruits. And likewise the mountains and stones, for their part, have their smoothness, transparency and colours proportionately more beautiful. Moreover, those gems that are treasured here, sardian stones, jaspers, emeralds and everything of

109e

110a

110b

110c

110d

110e the kind, are fragments of them. But there everything is like that, and more beautiful still than our gems. The cause of this is that those stones are pure, not eaten up and not damaged either, as the stones in our region have been by decomposition and brine thanks to the deposits which have accumulated here, and which bring about deformities and illnesses in stones, in earth, and in animals and plants too. The earth itself, however,

111a is decorated with all these, and besides with gold, silver and the other such metals. For they are by nature openly in sight, and they are many in number, large, and all over the earth. As a result, seeing the earth is a vision to make the viewer happy.

'On its surface there are animals of many kinds, including human beings, some of them dwelling inland, others dwelling around the air as we do around the sea, and yet others on islands which lie beside the mainland with air flowing around them. In short, the function served for

111b us by water and sea is served for them by air, and the function served for us by air is served for them by aether. Their seasons are balanced in such a way that they are free of illness and live for a much longer time than the people here; and in sight, hearing, wisdom, and all such things they exceed us in the same degree as air exceeds water in purity and aether air. Above all, they have groves and shrines of the gods, in which gods really are dwellers, and they have utterances, prophecies and sightings

111c of the gods, events which also occur in face-to-face meetings with them. Furthermore, the sun and moon and celestial bodies are seen by them as they really are, and their happiness in other ways too is in keeping with all this.

'Now the earth as a whole and the things surrounding the earth are of this nature. But there are regions in it, wherever it is hollowed, many of them around the whole earth in a ring, some of which are deeper and more gaping than the region in which we dwell, while others are deeper

111d but have a smaller mouth than the region around us, and there are others both shallower in depth and wider than the region here. All these regions open into each other underground by many routes, both narrower and wider, and have outlets running through them, by which a great amount of water flows back and forth between them, as if into mixing bowls. Beneath the earth there are unimaginably large ever-flowing rivers of both hot and cold waters, and a great amount of fire and large rivers of

111e fire, and many rivers of liquid mud, both of purer mud and of a more filthy sort, just as in Sicily there are rivers of mud flowing ahead of the lava and there is the lava itself. The regions are each filled with these, in whatever way the circuit happens to come to each of them each time. All these things are moved back and forth as if by a sort of oscillation inside the earth. And apparently this oscillation exists on account of a natural arrangement of the following kind.

'One of the chasms in the earth is in fact the largest in a number of ways, but in particular because it is bored right through the whole earth. This is the one Homer mentioned,[61] when he described it as:

112a

A long way away, where there is the deepest pit under the earth.

'Elsewhere both Homer[62] and many other poets have called it Tartarus. All the rivers flow together into this chasm and flow out of it again. And each river comes to be like the kind of earth through which it flows. The cause of all the streams flowing out from here, and flowing inside, is that this liquid has no base and no foundation. So it oscillates and surges back and forth, and the air and the wind around the liquid do the same. For they follow along with the liquid, both when it rushes towards the other side of the earth and when it rushes towards our side. Just as, when animals breathe, their breath is exhaled and inhaled in an unbroken flow, so too there the wind[63] oscillates with the liquid and brings about some formidable and unimaginable gales, both when the wind goes in and when it goes out.

112b

'Now whenever the water retreats into the region that is said to be "below", it flows through the earth into the places to which those streams lead, and, like people pumping, fills them. Again, whenever it empties from there and rushes back this way, it fills the streams here afresh; and when they are full they flow through the channels and through the earth, and each of them comes to the particular region into which its channel is formed, and they create seas, lakes, rivers and springs. From there they sink back down under the earth, some of them going around longer and more numerous tracts, others going around fewer and shorter ones, and then they fall into Tartarus again. In some cases this is far lower than where they were pumped out, in other cases only slightly lower; but they all do flow in lower than where they flow out, and some of them flow in directly opposite the place where they came out,[*64] while others do so in

112c

112d

---

[61] *Iliad* 8.14.   [62] *Iliad* 8.481.
[63] The same Greek word is used both for 'breath' and for 'wind'.
[*64] Omitting εἰσρεῖ at 112d5, with Stobaeus; see Verdenius, 'Notes on Plato's *Phaedo*'.

the same part. Now there are some that go all the way round in a circle, wound round the earth like snakes either once or even several times, and 112e then drop as far down as they can and fall back in. They can drop down in either direction as far as the middle, but no further; for the part on either side becomes steep for both the streams.

'The other streams are many, large and of every kind, and among these many streams there turn out to be four in particular, of which the one that is largest, and flows furthest outside and around in a circle, is the so-called Ocean. Directly opposite it, flowing in the opposite direction, is 113a Acheron, which flows through various barren regions, and in particular flows underground to reach the Acherusian lake. There the souls of most of those who have died come and stay for certain ordained times, longer in some cases, shorter in others, and then are sent away to be born as living creatures. A third river disgorges in the middle of these two and, close to its mouth, it comes out into a large region that is ablaze with a great amount of fire, and forms a lake larger than our sea, a lake bubbling 113b up with water and mud. From here it moves, squalid and muddy, in a circle, and, winding around inside the earth, comes to various places, including the edge of the Acherusian lake, though it does not mix with its water. After winding round many times underground, it falls into a lower part of Tartarus. This is the one they name "Pyriphlegethon", and scraps of it are blown out by the torrents of lava in various places on the earth. The fourth river comes out opposite it, initially into a 113c region that is frighteningly desolate, it is said, and a deep black colour all over. This is the region*[65] that they name "Stygian", and the river falls into and forms the lake "Styx".*[66] The river comes in here and receives formidable powers in the water, then it sinks under the earth and, as it winds round, moves in the opposite direction to the Pyriphlegethon and meets it in the Acherusian lake from the opposite side. Its water too does not mix with any other, but it likewise goes round in a circle and then falls into Tartarus opposite the Pyriphlegethon. Its name, the poets say, is Cocytus.

113d 'This then is the nature of the rivers. When the dead arrive, each in the region to which the spirit escorts it, they first present themselves in court, both those who lived nobly and piously and those who did not.

---

*[65] Reading ὃν δή rather than ὃ δή at 113c1.
*[66] Omitting ἣν at 113c2, with most MSS.

Those found to have lived average lives journey to the Acheron, and step onto certain things that serve them as rafts, and then on these they enter the lake. There they dwell and, if anyone has done anything wrong, they are purified by being punished for their wrongs, and so are pardoned; and they receive honours in recognition of their good deeds, each according 113e to his deserts. All those found to be incurable because of the gravity of their offences, who have committed either many grave sacrilegious acts, or many unjust and unlawful murders, or anything else that is of this kind, are flung by the fate they deserve into Tartarus, and never step out from there. But all those who are found guilty of curable but grave offences, for example, those who in a fit of anger acted violently to a father or mother and spent the rest of their lives regretting it, or those 114a who became homicides in similar circumstances, must be banished to Tartarus. When they have been banished and have spent a year there, the surge throws them out, sending the homicides down the Cocytus, and the father- and mother-beaters down the Pyriphlegethon. When their journey brings them alongside the Acherusian lake, here they shout and call, some calling to those they killed, others to those they injured. When they have called to them, they beg and beseech them to let them step 114b out into the lake, and to receive them. If they persuade them, out they step and their evils are over, but, if not, they are sent to Tartarus again, and from there back into the rivers. And this does not stop happening to them until they persuade those they wronged. For this is the punishment imposed on them by the jurors.

'But as for all those who are found to have lived exceptionally pious lives, they are the ones who are freed and separated from these regions inside the earth, as if from prisons, enter the pure dwelling above, and 114c make their dwelling on the earth's surface. And of these, those who purified themselves sufficiently with philosophy live thereafter entirely without bodies, and enter dwellings fairer still than these, although explaining these dwellings is not easy, nor is there sufficient time in the present circumstances. Anyhow, Simmias, the things we have described are the reason why we should do everything we can to have a share of virtue and wisdom in life. For fair is the prize and great the hope.

'Now it does not befit a man of intelligence to insist that these things 114d are as I have described them. However, since the soul turns out to be immortal, I think that for someone who believes this to be so it is both fitting and worth the risk – for fair is the risk – to insist that either what

I have said or something like it is true concerning our souls and their dwelling places. One must, so to speak, chant such things to oneself, which is why I myself have been drawing out my myth for a long time. Anyhow, these are the reasons why a man should be confident about his

114e own soul if he is one who in his life ignored the other pleasures, namely the bodily ones, and the body's adornments, as belonging to something else, because he believed that they bring about more harm than good, but pursued the pleasures of learning, and adorned his soul not with an adornment that belongs to something else, but with the soul's own

115a adornment,[67] namely temperance, justice, courage, freedom and truth, and thus awaits the journey to Hades as one who will make it whenever destiny calls. Now as for you, Simmias, Cebes and you others, you will each make the journey some time hereafter. But I am even now being called, as a man in a tragedy would say, by destiny. The hour has more or less come for me to turn to my bath; for it seems better to take a bath before drinking the poison, and so not to burden the women with the job of washing a corpse.'

115b   After Socrates had said this, Crito replied: 'Very well, Socrates. But what are your instructions, to these people or to me, concerning either your children or anything else? I mean whatever would be the greatest favour we can do you.'

'Just what I always say, Crito' he said, 'and nothing particularly new. That is, that if you take care of yourselves, whatever you do will be a favour to me and mine, and to yourselves, even if you don't undertake to do so now. If on the other hand you fail to take care of yourselves, and refuse to live by following the trail set by today's conversation and our

115c previous ones, then however many firm undertakings you make now, you won't do any good.'

'Then we'll strive to do so,' he said. 'And how should we bury you?'

'However you want,' he said, 'as long as you catch me and I don't escape you.' As he said this he laughed gently and looked towards us, then said: 'Gentlemen, I'm not convincing Crito that I am Socrates here, the one who is now holding a conversation – setting out remarks one

115d by one. Instead he supposes that I'm that corpse which he'll shortly be seeing, and he actually asks how he should bury me. As for the argument I have spent a long time propounding, that when I drink the poison I

[67] The same Greek word is used both for 'adornment' and for the soul's 'composure'.

won't stay behind in your company any longer, but will depart and be gone to some happy state fit for the blessed, I seem to be wasting my breath on him, while reassuring both you and myself. So you must give surety for me to Crito,' he said, 'the opposite surety to the one Crito tried to give my jurors. For he guaranteed that I *would* stay behind, but you must give surety that I will *not* stay behind when I die, but will depart   115e
and be gone. That way Crito can bear it more readily, and, when he sees my body being either burned or buried, need not be upset on my behalf as if terrible things were happening to me, or say at the funeral that it is Socrates that he is laying out, or carrying to the tomb, or burying. For you need to understand, my excellent Crito,' he said, 'that not speaking correctly is not just a travesty of the point at issue, but also has a bad effect on people's souls. No, you should cheerfully say that you're burying my body, and you should bury it in whatever way you like and consider most   116a
in accordance with the rules.'

After saying this he stood up and went into a room to take a bath. Crito went with him, but told us to wait. So we waited, and as we did so we held a conversation amongst ourselves on the things that had been said, and considered them again; but for some of the time we spelled out how great a misfortune had befallen us, for we really thought that it was as if we were about to lose our father and spend the rest of our lives as orphans. When he had taken his bath and his children had been brought   116b
to him – he had two small sons and one older one – and those women of his household had come, he had a conversation with them in front of Crito and instructed them to do various things he wanted, and then told the women and children to leave. Then he came over to us on his own. It was already nearly sunset, as he had spent a long time inside. He came and sat down, freshly bathed, and after that there was only a brief conversation before the servant of the Eleven[68] arrived and came over to him. 'Socrates,' he said, 'I won't bring against you the charge that I   116c
bring against others, that they get angry with me and call down curses whenever I bring them the command, enforced by the authorities, that they must drink the poison. I've come to know in other ways too during this time that you're the noblest, kindest and best man ever to come here. And now in particular I'm quite sure that you aren't angry with me, for you know the people to blame, and are angry with them. So now,

[68] See n. 7 above.

116d   since you know what I've come to tell you, goodbye, and try to bear the inevitable as best you can.' He promptly burst into tears, then turned and left.

Socrates looked up towards him and said: 'Goodbye to you too, and we'll do as you say.' With that he said to us: 'What a courteous person! Throughout all my time here he's been visiting, sometimes stopping for a conversation, and he's been the most likeable of men. How decent it is of him to cry for me now. But come, Crito, let us heed his words, and let someone bring the poison, if it's ready and ground. If not, the man had better grind it.'

116e   To which Crito said: 'But, Socrates, I think that the sun is still on the mountains and hasn't set yet. On top of that, I know that others too drink the poison long after the command has come to them, and first have a good dinner and a good deal to drink and, what's more, some first have sex with whoever they happen to desire. But don't hurry at all – there's still time.'

Socrates then said: 'Yes, Crito, the people you mention do these things with good reason – they think that they gain from having done them, you

117a   see – and I myself won't do these things, likewise with good reason. For I think I'll gain nothing from having drunk it a little later, except making myself a laughing-stock in my own eyes by clinging to life, and by being tight-fisted when there's nothing left to keep. No, come on,' he said, 'do as I say and don't refuse.'

When Crito heard that he nodded to his slave, who was standing nearby. The slave went out, and after a long time came back with the man who was going to administer the poison, who brought it ready and ground in a cup. When Socrates saw the man, he said: 'Very well, my excellent friend. You're the expert. What should I do?'

117b   'Just drink it and then walk around,' he said, 'until a heaviness comes in your legs. Then lie down, and it will take effect by itself.' With that he handed Socrates the cup.

Socrates took it very gladly indeed, Echecrates, without any fear and with no change to either his colour or his expression. Eying the man with a characteristically mischievous look, he said: 'What would you say about pouring a libation from this drink in someone's honour? Is it allowed or not?'

'We grind only as much as we think is the right amount to drink, Socrates,' he said.

'I understand,' he said. 'But it is surely both allowed and right to *pray* 117c
to the gods that the change of dwelling from here to there may be attended
by good fortune. That is what I pray, and so may it happen.'

As soon as he'd said this, he held the cup to his lips and drank it all,
utterly coolly and contentedly. So far most of us had been pretty much
able to hold back our tears, but when we saw him drinking and draining
it, we couldn't do so any longer, but at least in my case the tears came
flooding out in spite of myself, and so I covered my head and wept for
myself – not for him, you understand, but for my own fortune, that I'd 117d
lost such a friend. Already before me, Crito, when he couldn't hold back
his tears, had stood up and walked away. But Apollodorus hadn't stopped
crying for a moment even previously, and now he howled out as he wept
and lamented, and got the whole group in tears, apart from Socrates
himself.

Socrates said: 'You astonish me – what a way for you all to behave!
You realize it was not least for this reason that I sent away the women, so
that they wouldn't strike the wrong note in this sort of way. For in fact 117e
I've heard that one should meet one's end in a reverent silence. No, keep
quiet and show some resolve.'

When we heard this, we felt ashamed of ourselves and stopped crying.
But Socrates walked around, and then, when he said that his legs were
heavy, lay down on his back, as the man was telling him to do. As soon
as he did so, this man*69 took hold of him, and after a while examined
Socrates' feet and legs, then gave his foot a hard pinch and asked if he 118a
felt it. Socrates said he didn't. Next he did the same again to Socrates'
shins, and by going up the body in this way he showed us that Socrates
was going cold and rigid. The man kept hold of him and said that, when
it reached his heart, he would then be gone.

By now it was pretty much the parts around his abdomen that were
going cold, when he uncovered his head – as it had been covered – and
said his last words: 'Crito, we owe a cock to Asclepius. All70 of you must
pay the debt and not overlook it.'

'Yes, that will be done,' said Crito. 'But see if you have something else
to say.'

---

*69 Deleting ὁ δοὺς τὸ φάρμακον (117e6–7) with Verdenius, 'Notes on Plato's *Phaedo*'.
70 'All' is added in the translation to convey the fact that Socrates uses the second person plural,
speaking to the whole group and not to Crito alone. They all share this mysterious debt, and it
is for all the survivors to repay it.

To this question Socrates gave no further answer, but after a little while he moved, and the man uncovered him. His eyes went fixed. When Crito saw this, he closed the mouth and eyes.

That, Echecrates, was the end of our friend, a man who was, as we would say, the best of those whom we came to know in those days, and also the wisest and most just.

Index

117

Cambridge texts in the history of philosophy

Titles published in the series thus far

Aquinas *Disputed Questions on the Virtues* (edited by E. M. Atkins and Thomas Williams)
Aquinas *Summa Theologiae, Questions on God* (edited by Brian Davies and Brian Leftow)
Aristotle *Nicomachean Ethics* (edited by Roger Crisp)
Arnauld and Nicole *Logic or the Art of Thinking* (edited by Jill Vance Buroker)
Augustine *On the Free Choice of the Will, On Grace and Free Choice, and Other Writings* (edited by Peter King)
Augustine *On the Trinity* (edited by Gareth Matthews)
Bacon *The New Organon* (edited by Lisa Jardine and Michael Silverthorne)
Berkeley, *Philosophical Writings* (edited by Desmond M. Clarke)
Boyle *A Free Enquiry into the Vulgarly Received Notion of Nature* (edited by Edward B. Davis and Michael Hunter)
Bruno *Cause, Principle and Unity and Essays on Magic* (edited by Richard Blackwell and Robert de Lucca with an introduction by Alfonso Ingegno)
Cavendish *Observations upon Experimental Philosophy* (edited by Eileen O'Neill)
Cicero *On Moral Ends* (edited by Julia Annas, translated by Raphael Woolf)
Clarke *A Demonstration of the Being and Attributes of God and Other Writings* (edited by Ezio Vailati)
Classic and Romantic German Aesthetics (edited by J. M. Bernstein)
Condillac *Essay on the Origin of Human Knowledge* (edited by Hans Aarsleff)
Conway *The Principles of the Most Ancient and Modern Philosophy* (edited by Allison P. Coudert and Taylor Corse)
Cudworth *A Treatise Concerning Eternal and Immutable Morality with A Treatise of Freewill* (edited by Sarah Hutton)
Descartes *Meditations on First Philosophy, with selections from the Objections and Replies* (edited by John Cottingham)
Descartes *The World and Other Writings* (edited by Stephen Gaukroger)
Fichte *Attempt at a Critique of All Revelation* (edited by Allen Wood, translated by Garrett Green)
Fichte *Foundations of Natural Right* (edited by Frederick Neuhouser, translated by Michael Baur)
Fichte *The System of Ethics* (edited by Daniel Breazeale and Günter Zöller)
Greek and Roman Aesthetics (edited by Oleg V. Bychkov and Anne Sheppard)
Hamann *Philosophical Writings* (edited by Kenneth Haynes)
Heine *On the History of Religion and Philosophy in Germany and Other Writings* (edited by Terry Pinkard, translated by Howard Pollack-Milgate)
Herder *Philosophical Writings* (edited by Michael Forster)
Hobbes and Bramhall on Liberty and Necessity (edited by Vere Chappell)
Humboldt *On Language* (edited by Michael Losonsky, translated by Peter Heath)
Hume *Dialogues Concerning Natural Religion and Other Writings* (edited by Dorothy Coleman)

Nietzsche *Untimely Meditations* (edited by Daniel Breazeale, translated by R. J. Hollingdale)

Nietzsche *Writings from the Early Notebooks* (edited by Raymond Geuss and Alexander Nehamas, translated by Ladislaus Löb)

Nietzsche *Writings from the Late Notebooks* (edited by Rüdiger Bittner, translated by Kate Sturge)

Novalis *Fichte Studies* (edited by Jane Kneller)

Plato *Meno* and *Phaedo* (edited by David Sedley and Alex Long)

Plato *The Symposium* (edited by M.C. Howatson and Frisbee C. C. Sheffield)

Reinhold *Letters on the Kantian Philosophy* (edited by Karl Ameriks, translated by James Hebbeler)

Schleiermacher *Hermeneutics and Criticism* (edited by Andrew Bowie)

Schleiermacher *Lectures on Philosophical Ethics* (edited by Robert Louden, translated by Louise Adey Huish)

Schleiermacher *On Religion: Speeches to its Cultured Despisers* (edited by Richard Crouter)

Schopenhauer *Prize Essay on the Freedom of the Will* (edited by Günter Zöller)

Sextus Empiricus *Against the Logicians* (edited by Richard Bett)

Sextus Empiricus *Outlines of Scepticism* (edited by Julia Annas and Jonathan Barnes)

Shaftesbury *Characteristics of Men, Manners, Opinions, Times* (edited by Lawrence Klein)

Adam Smith *The Theory of Moral Sentiments* (edited by Knud Haakonssen)

Spinoza *Theological-Political Treatise* (edited by Jonathan Israel, translated by Michael Silverthorne and Jonathan Israel)

Voltaire *Treatise on Tolerance and Other Writings* (edited by Simon Harvey)

Printed in the United States
By Bookmasters